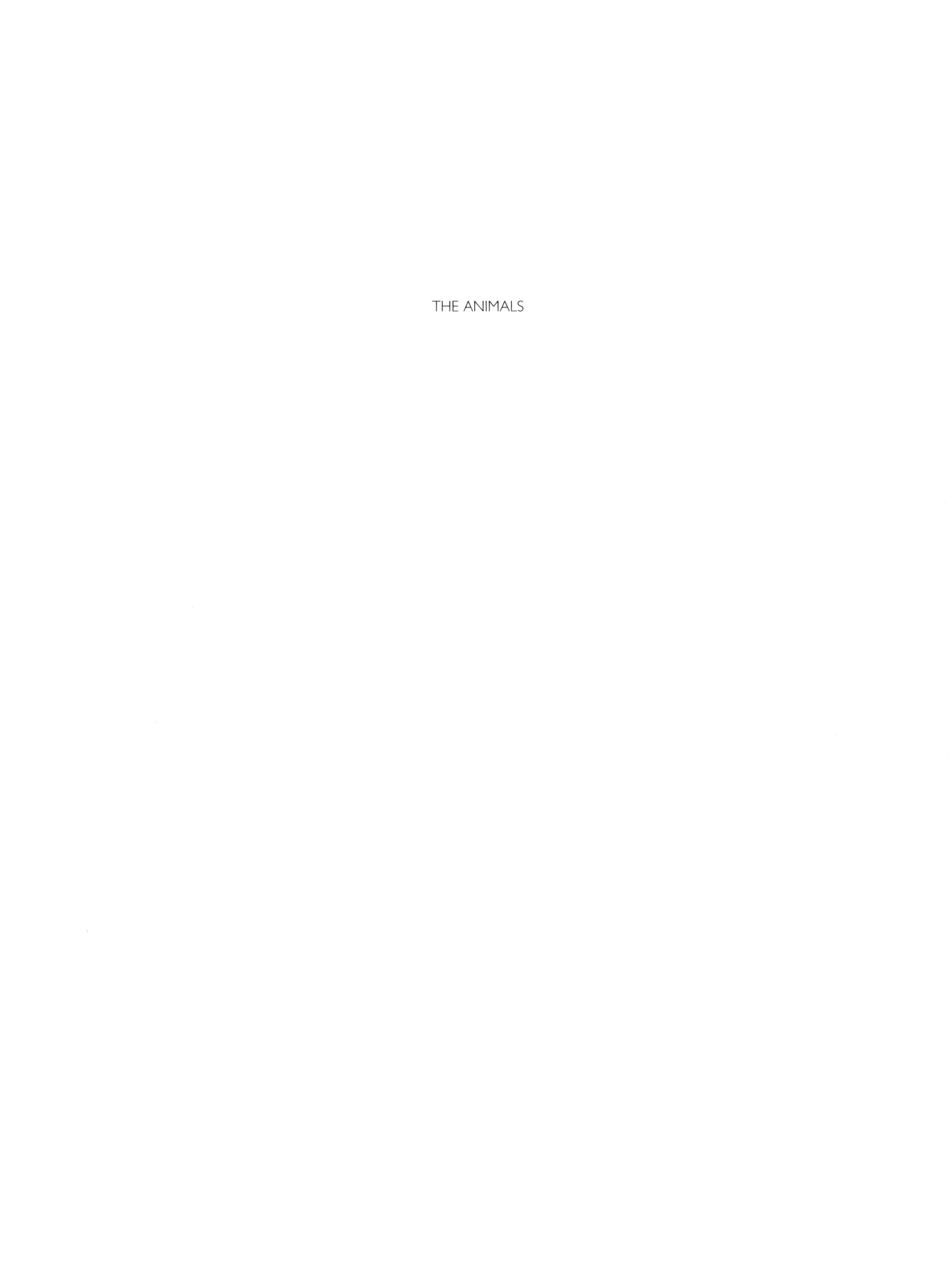

THE ANIMALS

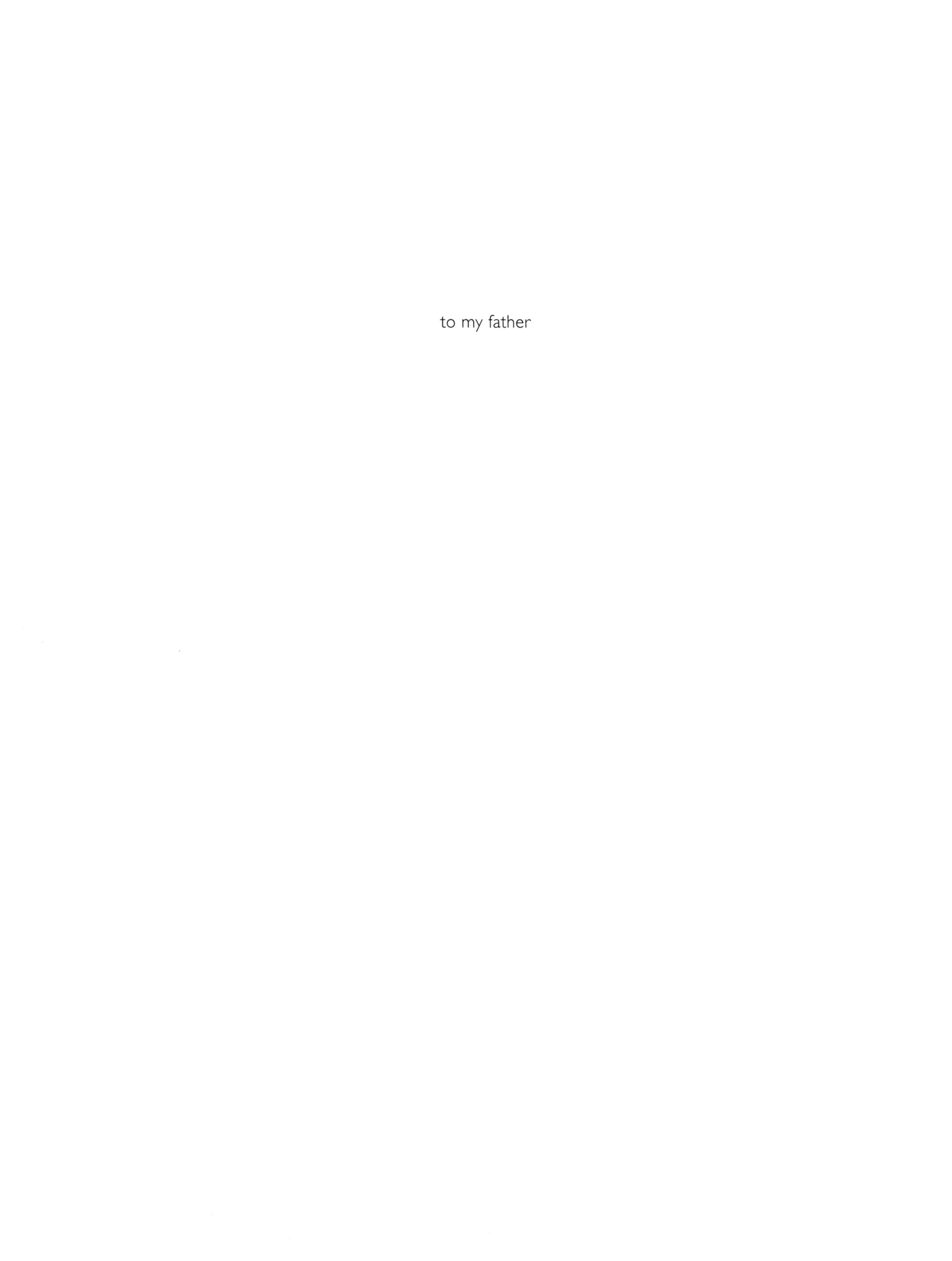

to my father

GIACOMO BRUNELLI
THE ANIMALS

introduction by
ALISON NORDSTRÖM

dewi lewis publishing

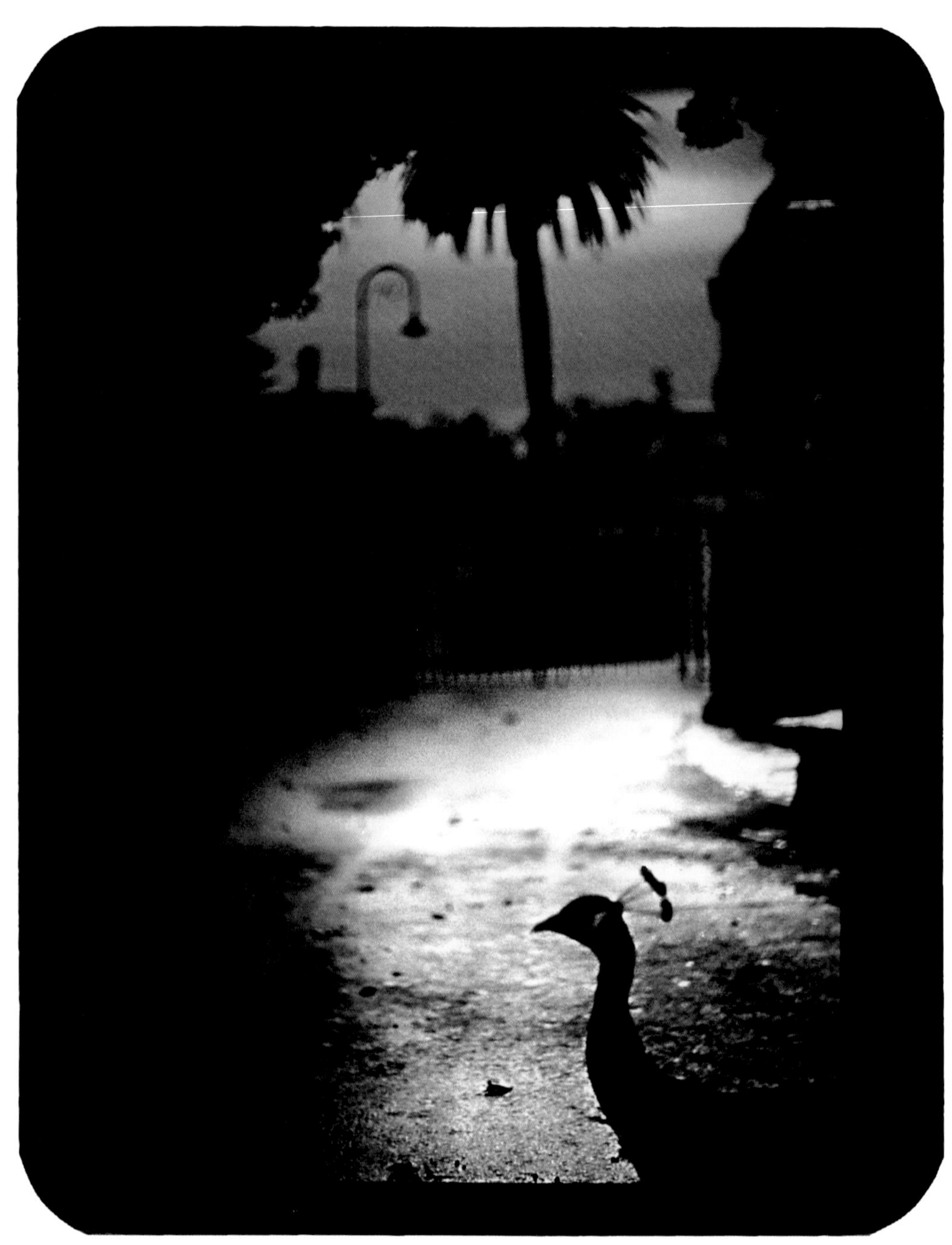

n his seminal 1980 essay *Why Look at Animals?* John Berger describes a dual, but not in any way contradictory, human-animal relationship: *'They belonged there and here. Likewise they were mortal and immortal. They were subjected and worshipped, bred and sacrificed.'* He asserts that the physical and temporal removal of animals from most of our lives has come with the rise of capitalism, the spread of industrialisation and the end of peasantry, but that the power of animals as metaphor, mystery and elemental spirit remains. For Berger, animals are the quintessential Other, and we look at them to define and discover ourselves.

Giacomo Brunelli has been looking hard at animals. His focus is not on the framed and caged exotica of zoos but on the ordinary animals that remain with us to some extent: horses, dogs, cats, chickens, pigeons. He shows us a fox, looking sharply at the camera and poised to flee, and there are numerous birds, a snake and several toads, but this wildness is small and fragile, living in the familiar liminal space where man-made and natural meet and overlap. His animals inhabit farmyards, cobbled streets and the façades of stone buildings. There are no tigers here.

Brunelli's animals are often composed only of suggestive fragments. His spare black and white images are attuned to the nuances of a moving mane, a silhouetted whisker, a highlighted, almost illuminated wing. He favours the profile and the counter-intuitive angle, setting dark unobservable features against dark undiscernable back-grounds. A dead mouse, on its back, paws in air beside an oversized flower against a stark and distant mountain is no more or less frozen in time than is the growling dog, eyes alight and teeth forever bared; both are icons of states we fear but cannot know. These pictures are timeless and uncanny, powerful in their ordinariness, and emotionally much bigger than their simple subjects. In them we find scraps of barely remembered troubled dreams, or even the barely retained remnants of that first consciousness that informed ancestral hands and minds in the caves of Chauvet-Pont-d'Arc and Lascaux some 30,000 years ago.

There is a strong implication of apocalypse in the intensity of lighting and setting of these curious and compelling images. In one, a white horse pulls itself upright from a prone position against a glowering sky horizoned by a dense line of indistinguishable trees. It is all powerful muscular flanks and determined muzzle, clearly something more than a horse in a field but nothing that can be kenned by intellect. That same ominous sky appears again behind a stretching, possibly snarling, housecat, the edge of its forepaw lit, its head and whiskers minimally picked out by the light, while black trees loom and clouds gather from the thick black border that establishes the image as a primal monster. Similarly, an ambiguous quadrapedal skeleton crouches in perpetuity against a barely visible backdrop of mountain and fog. We recognise it as animal and as dead, but that is all. These are creatures of darkness emerging from darkness; we know them but we do not know what they mean.

Pictures in a book may convey only part of the material nature and tactile experience of the photographs they represent. It is important to note here that Brunelli has chosen to keep his black-bordered pictures small and to round their corners like those of a nineteenth century cabinet card. They are, thus, intimate and contemplative, set in a distinctive universe altogether separate from the epic oversized colour work so prevalent today. They are secret and magical, with the power and intensity of totem, fetish, myth. They are quiet little stories that we tell ourselves because we have always known them. They fit our hands.

Brunelli's black and white images are straightforward but not uncomplicated and, taken together, they demonstrate the magical ability of the photograph both to trace and transform what we see. They show us what something looks like, asserting unquestionably that this is a horse's eye, a dog's neck, or the stance of a swan, but they also transcend this factual specificity to tap into something huge, persistent and ineffable. The success of these pictures is not in the information they provide, though the artist's visual delight in such information may be the source of his strength and consistency. These pictures work because they take us past information to emotion, both the artist's and our own, and perhaps past emotion to something else that embodies both the fascination and the fear of being part of the world we inhabit.

Alison Nordström

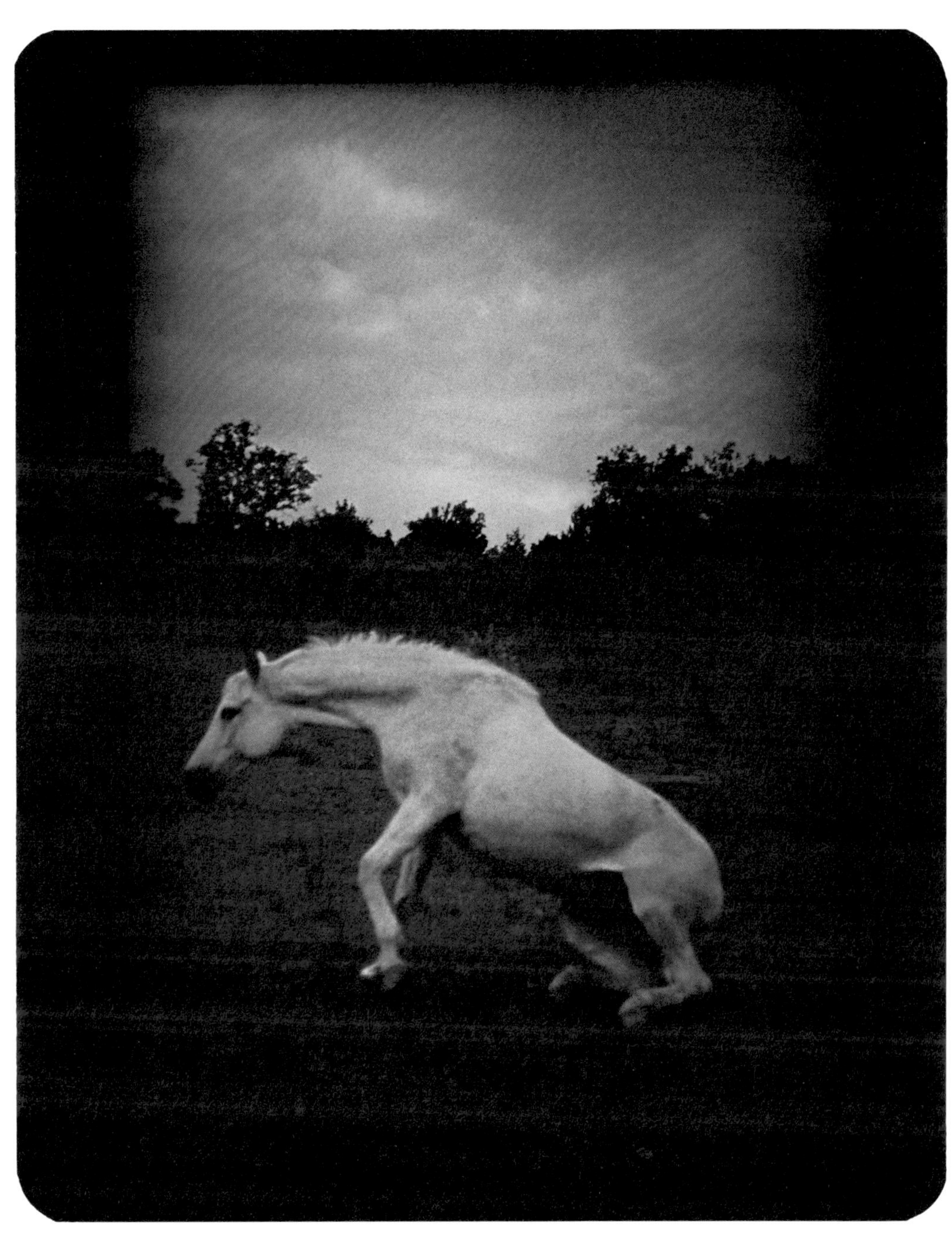

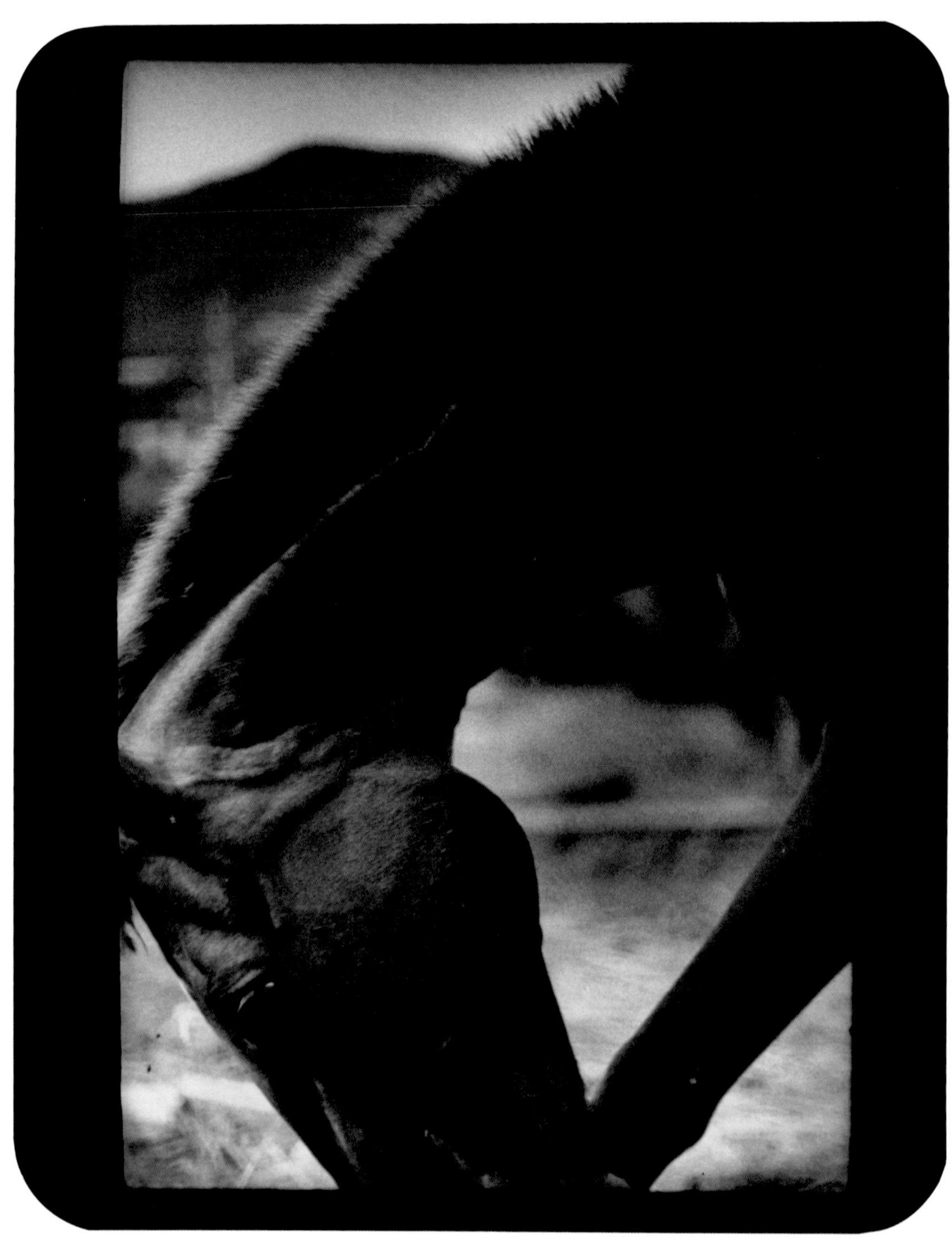

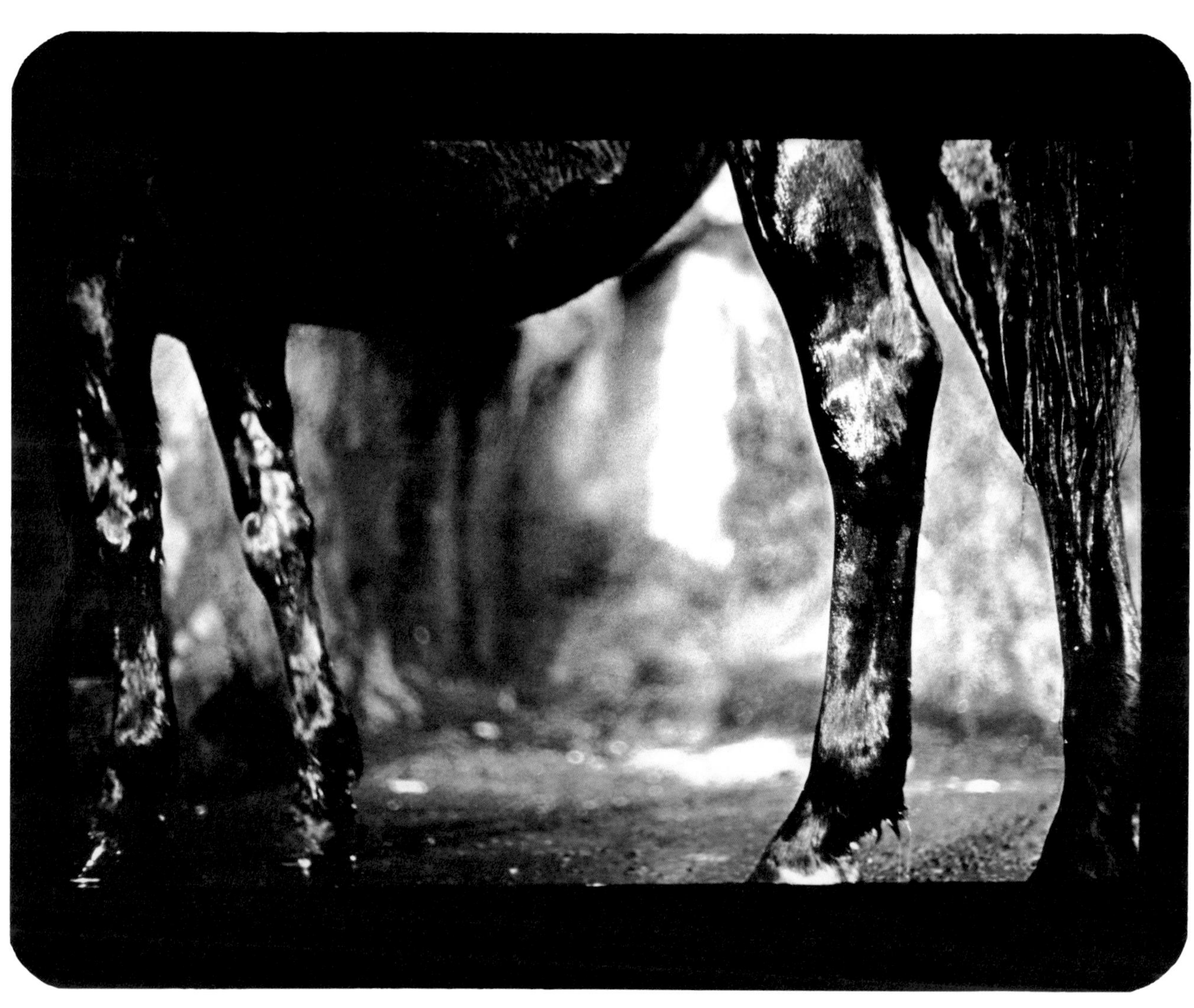

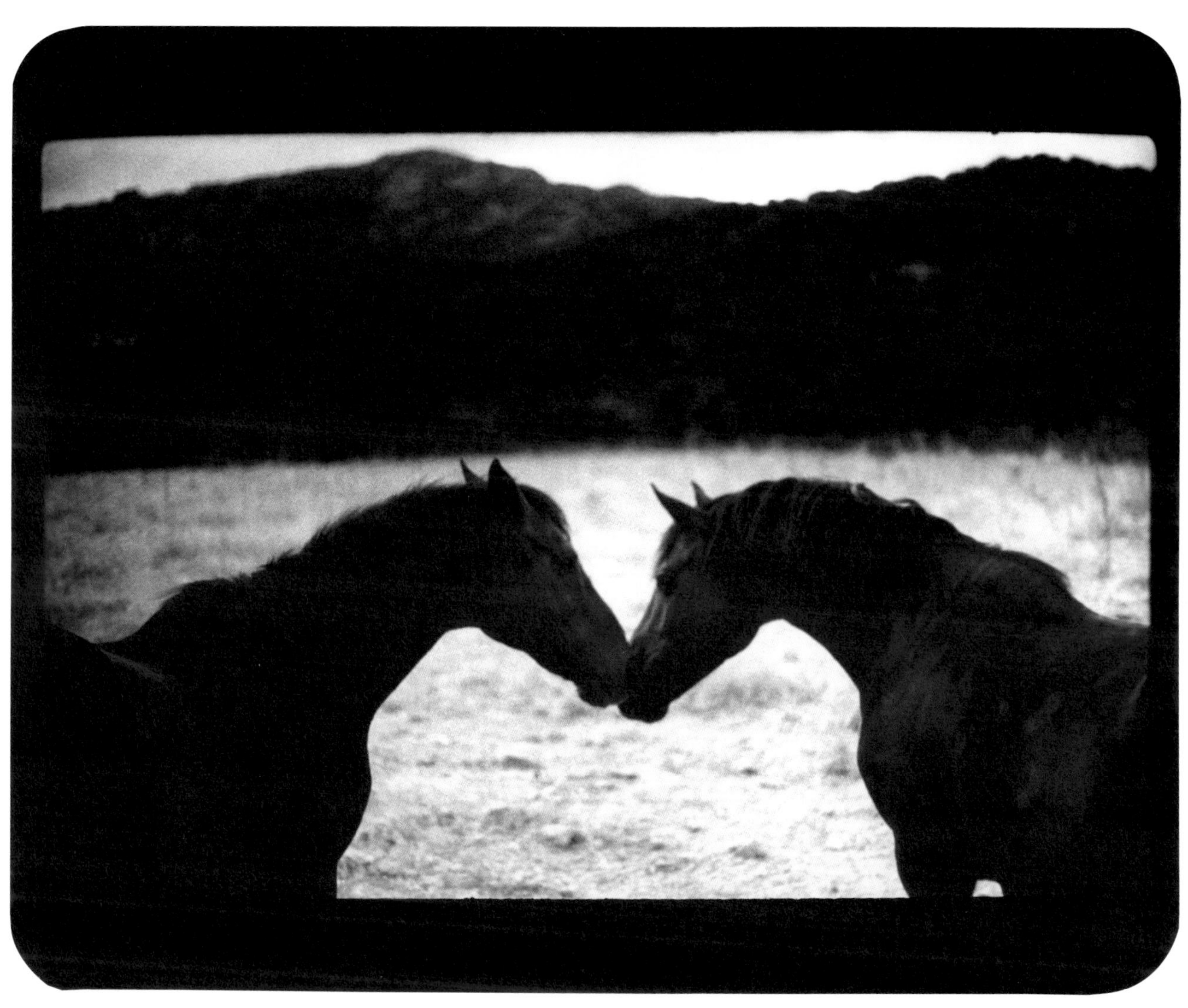

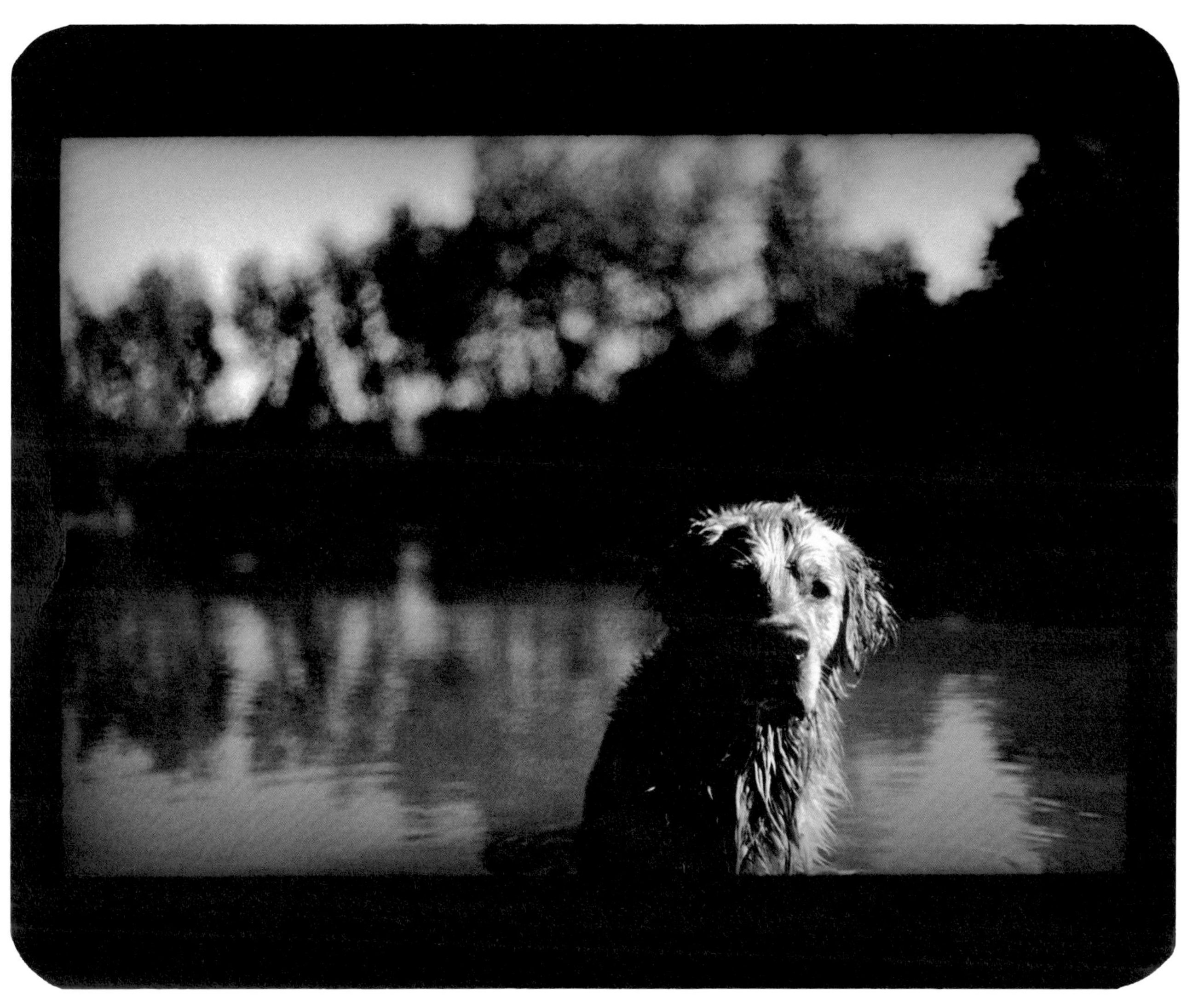

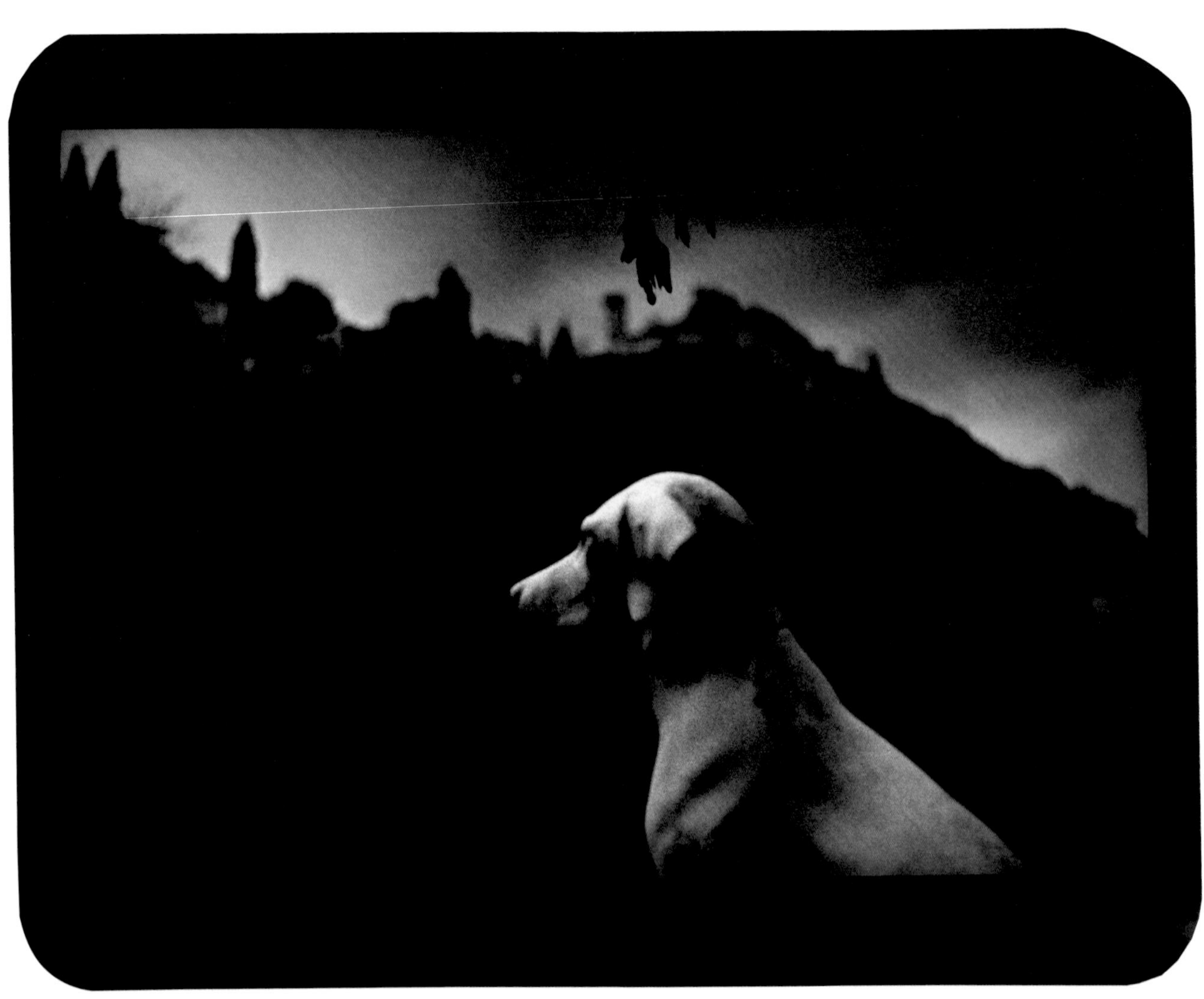

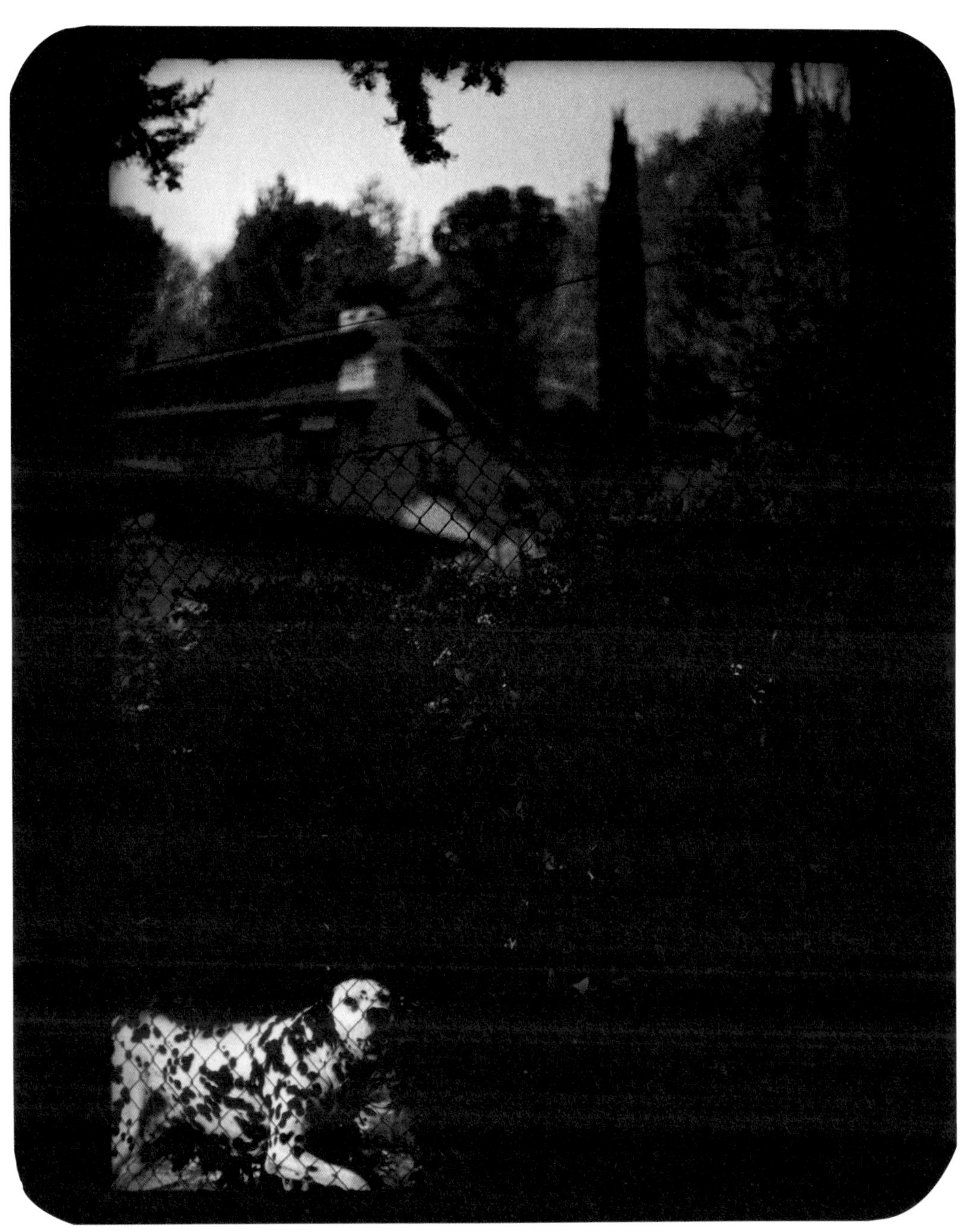

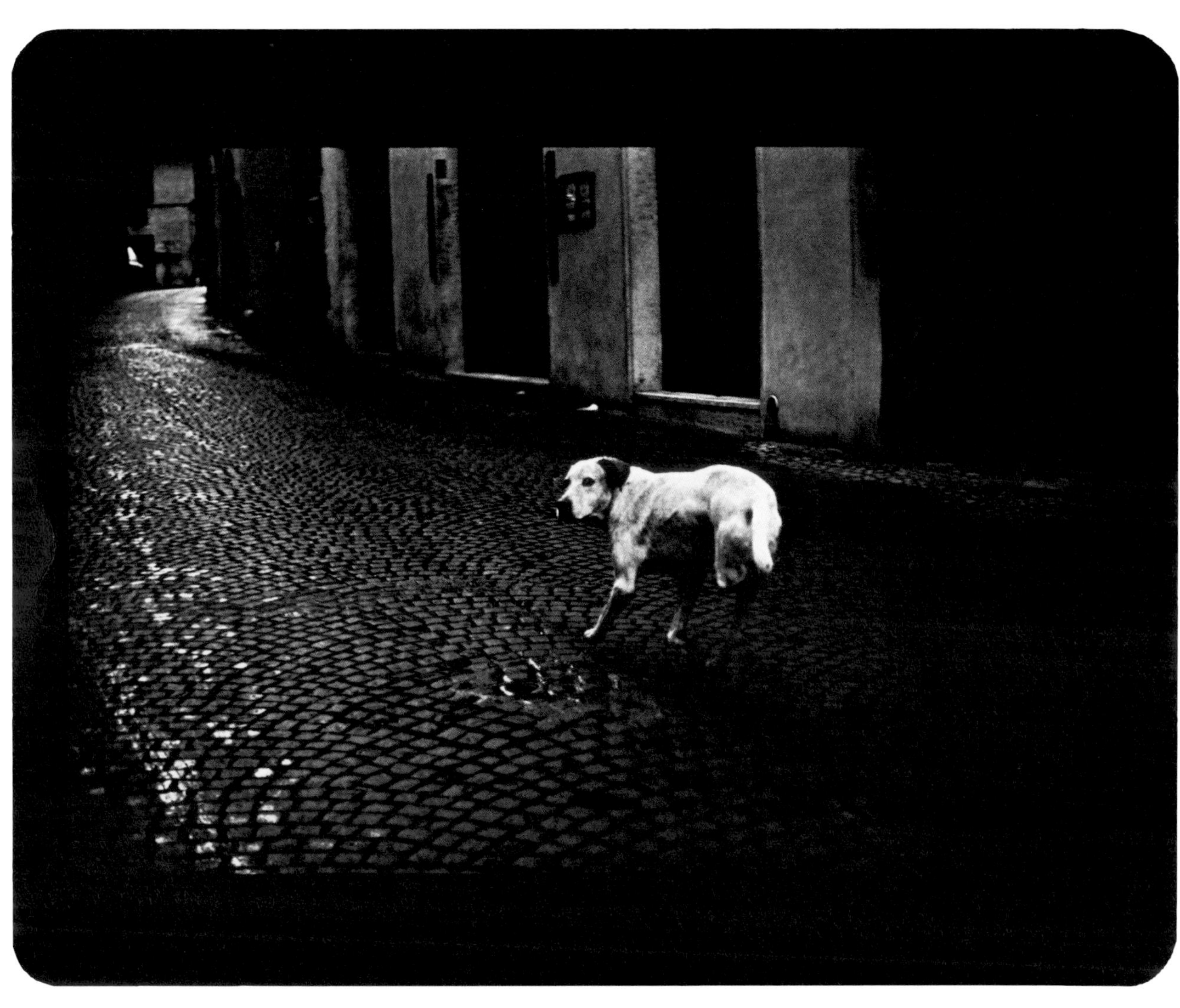

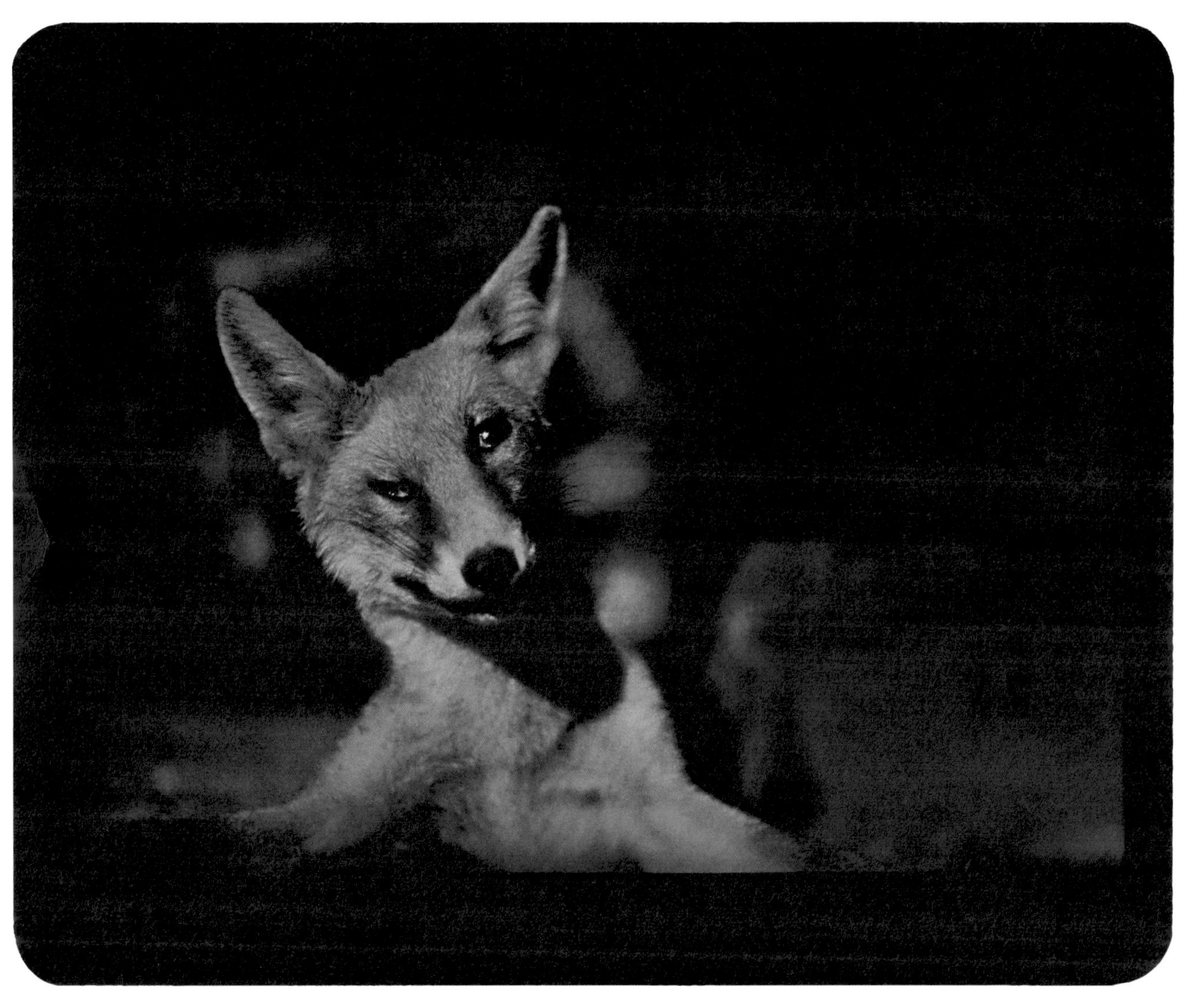

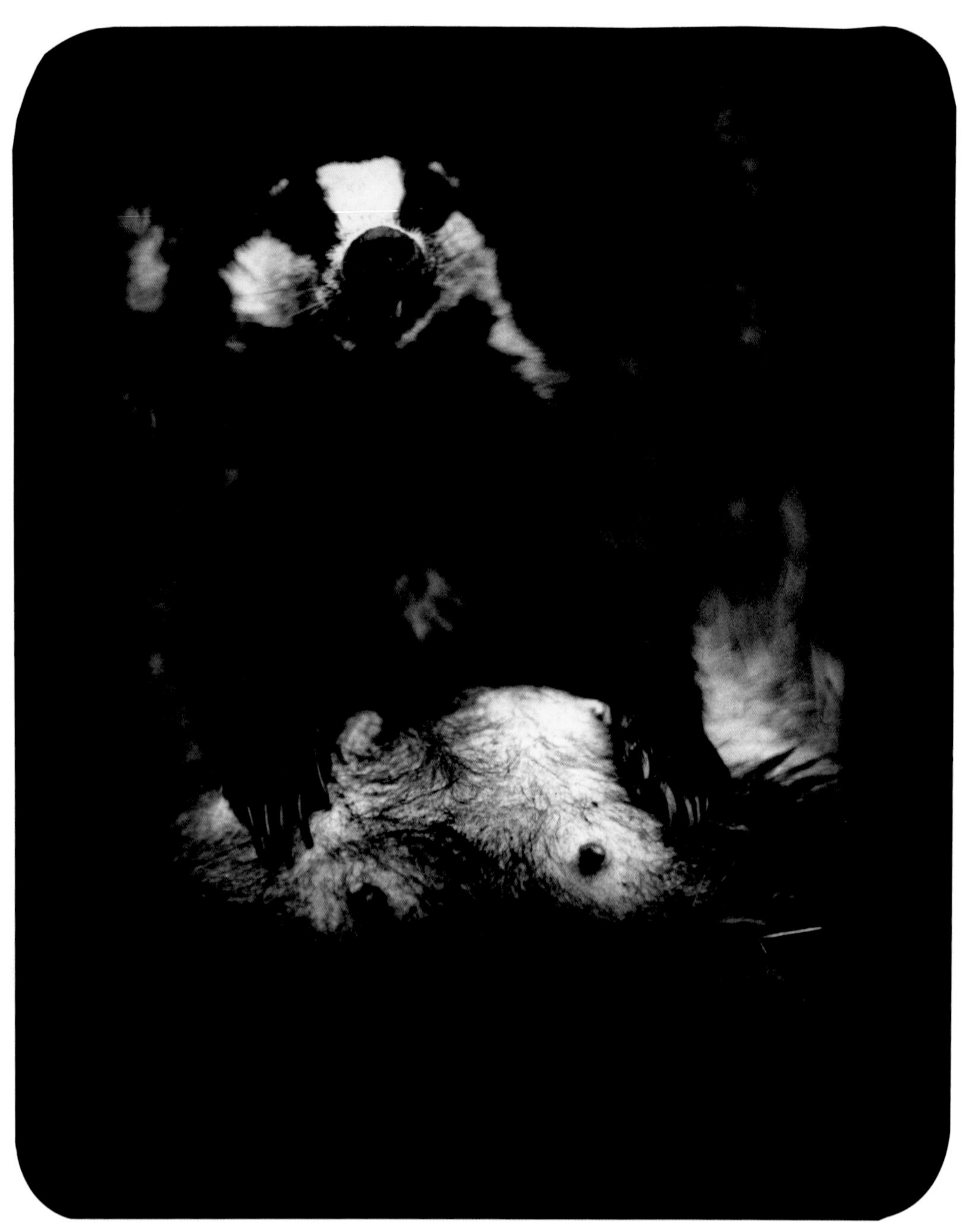

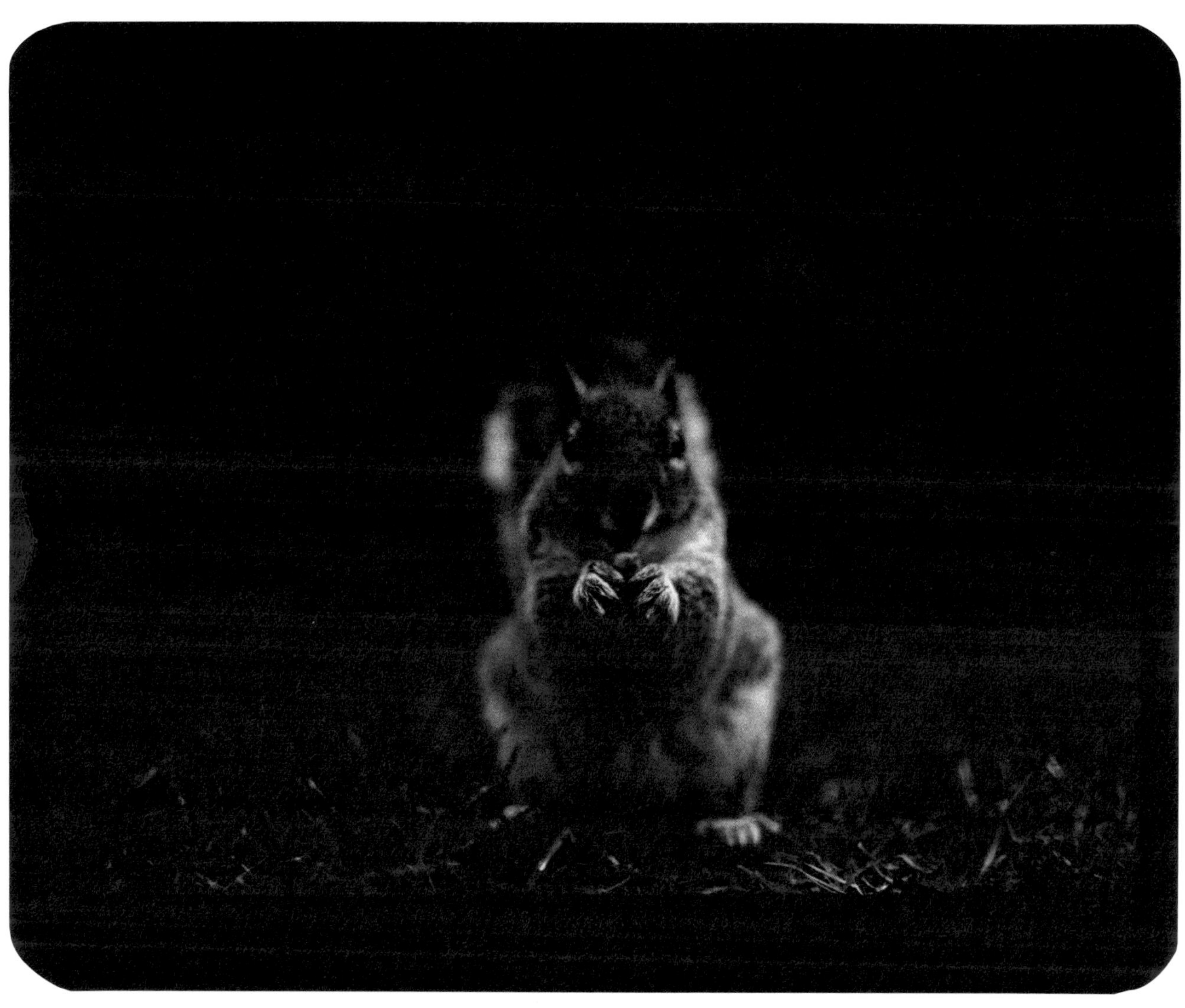

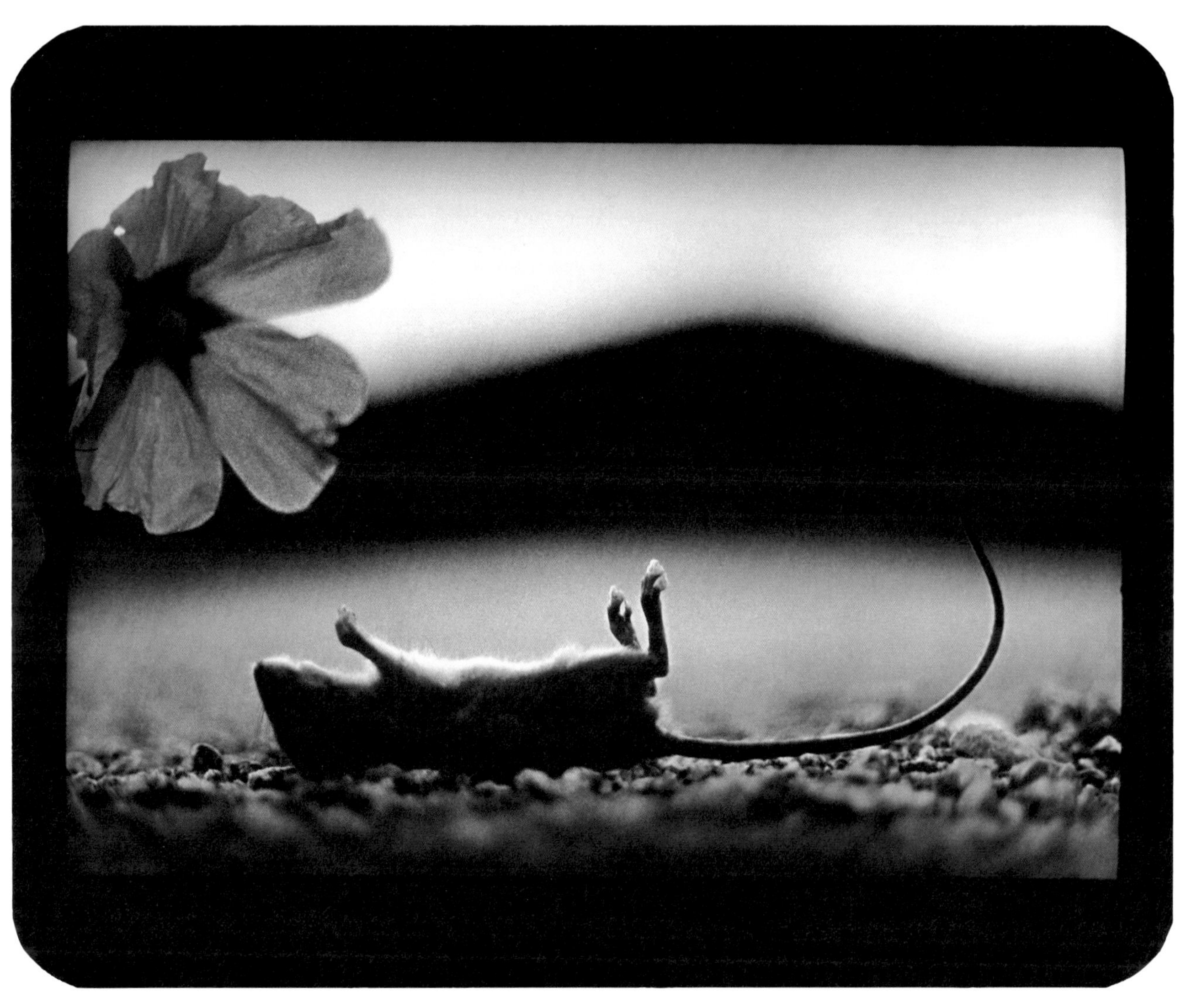

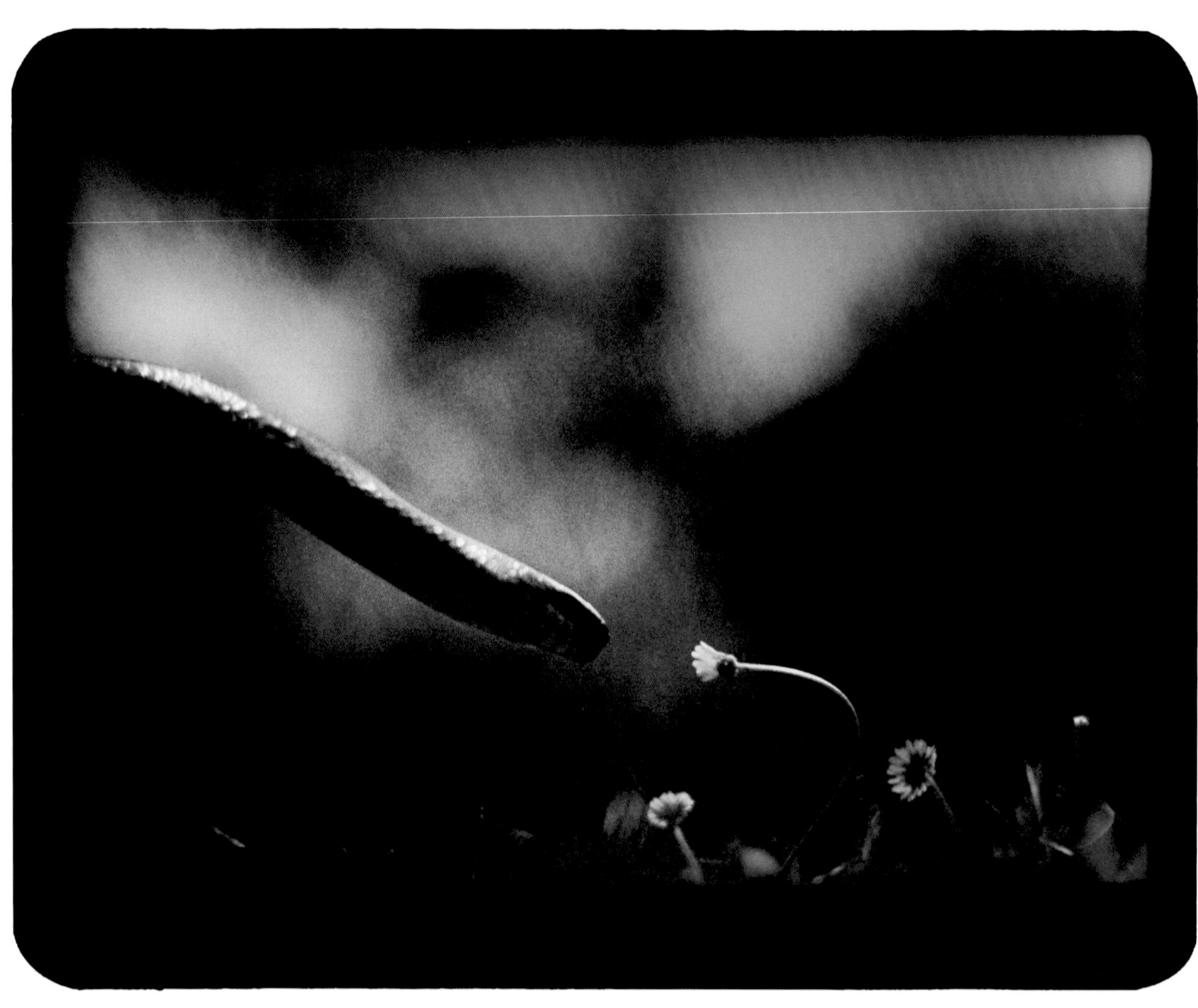

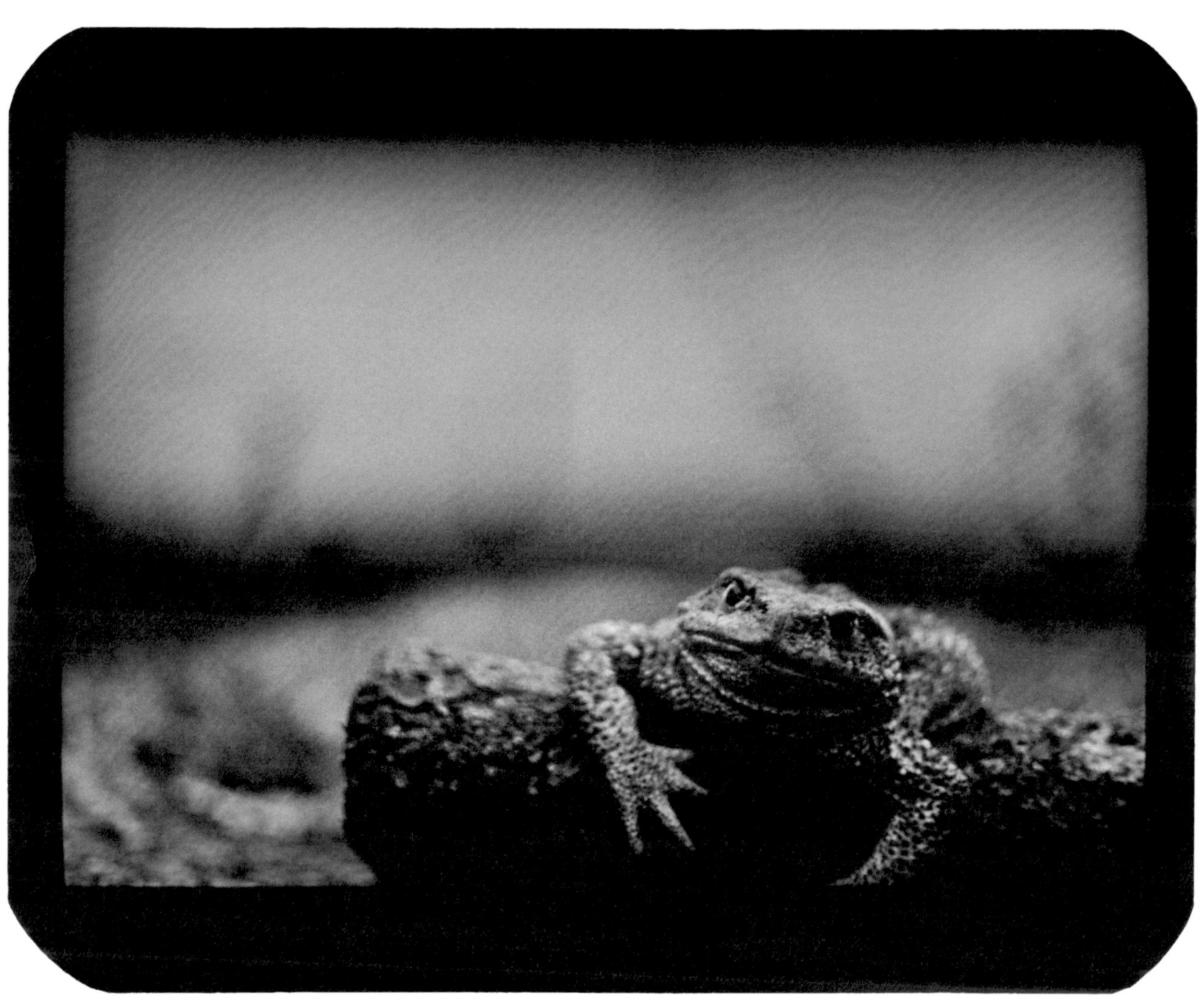

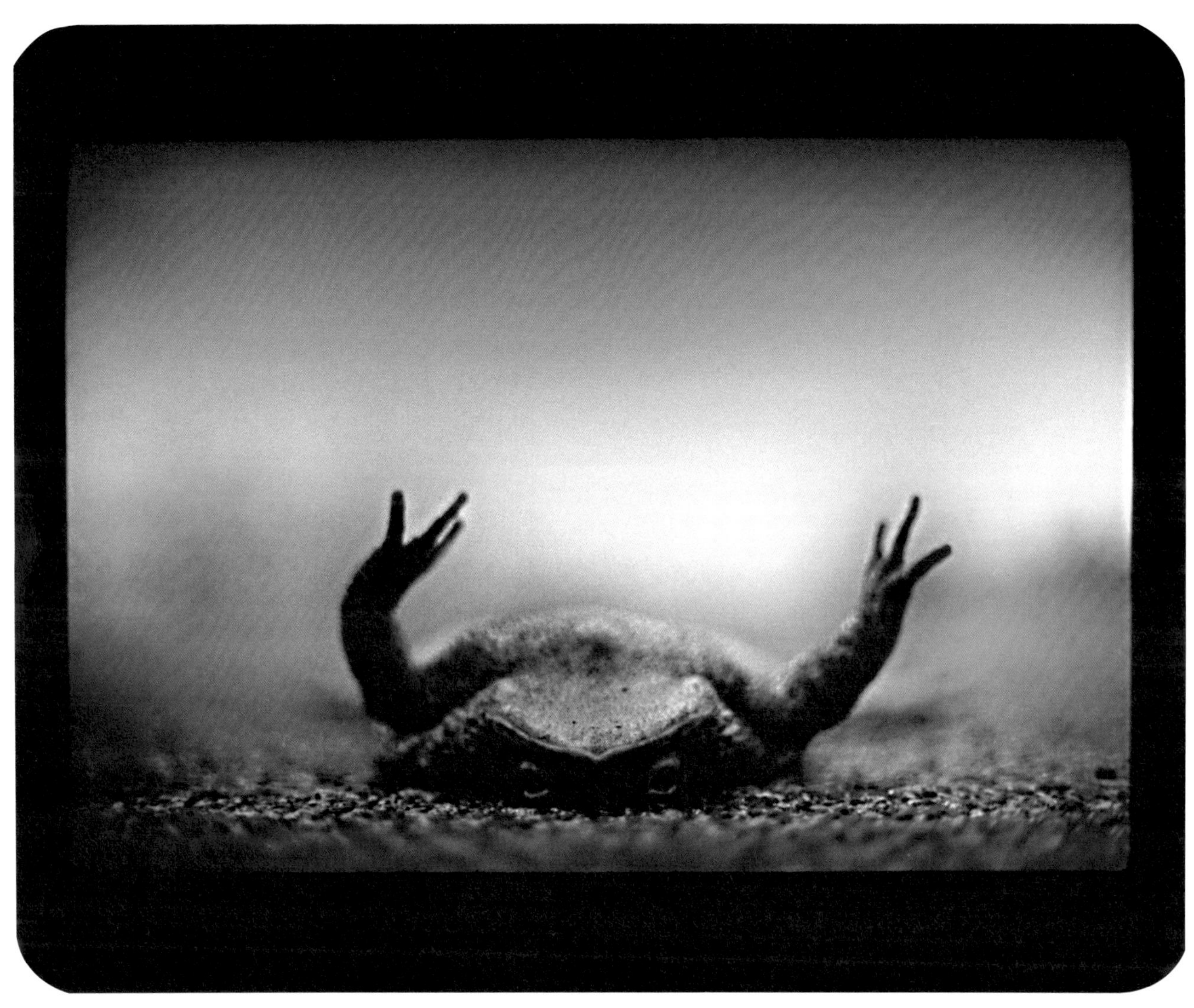

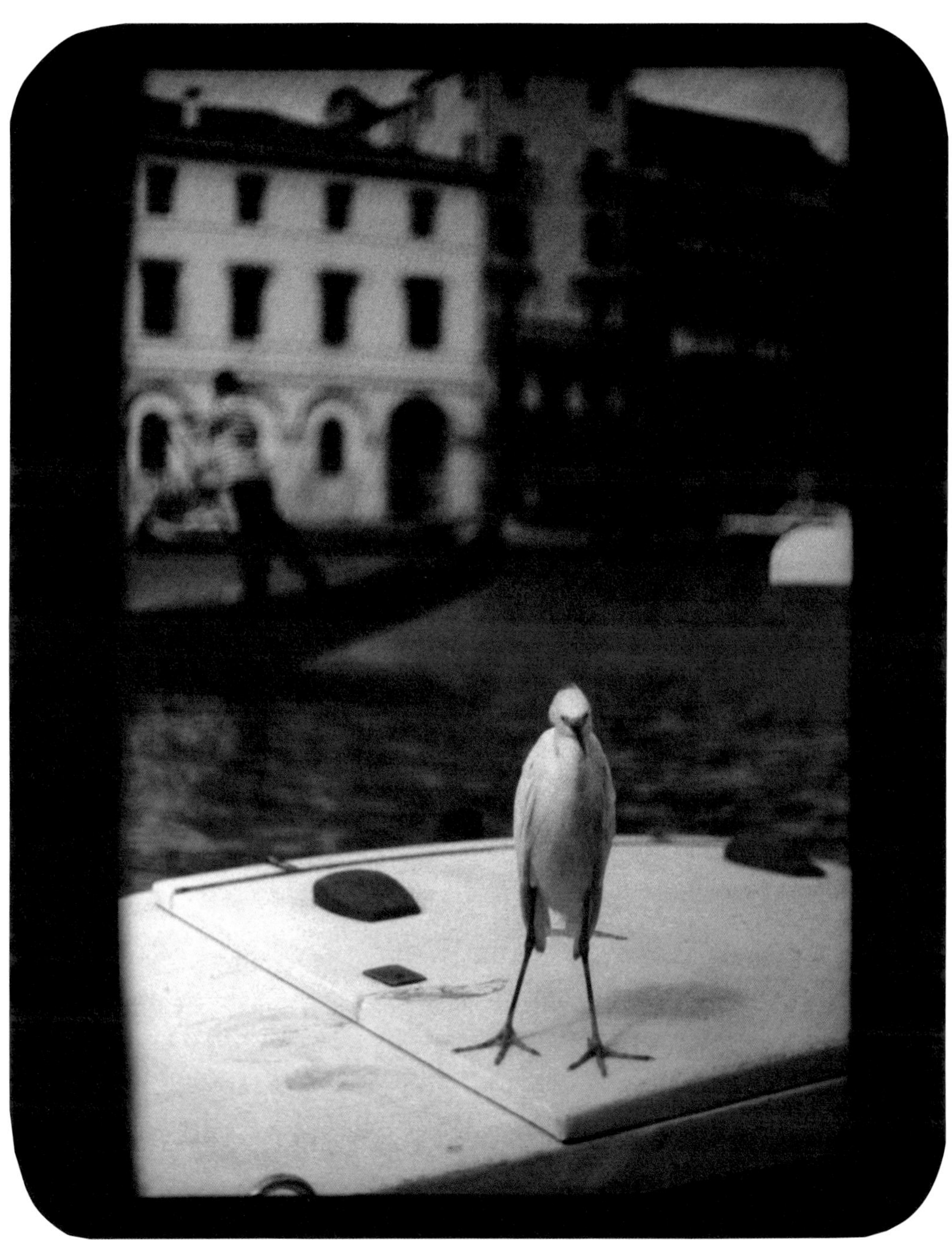

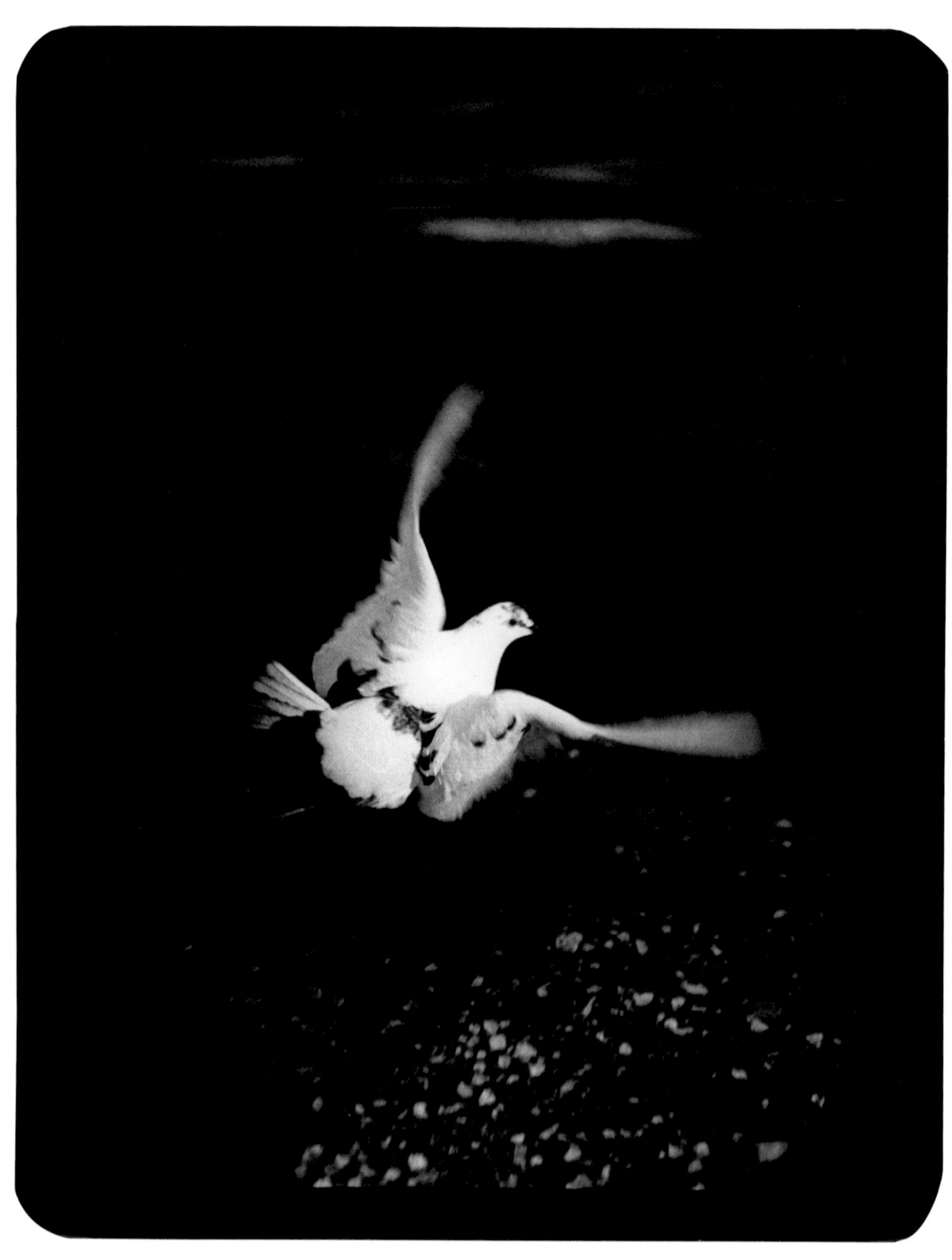

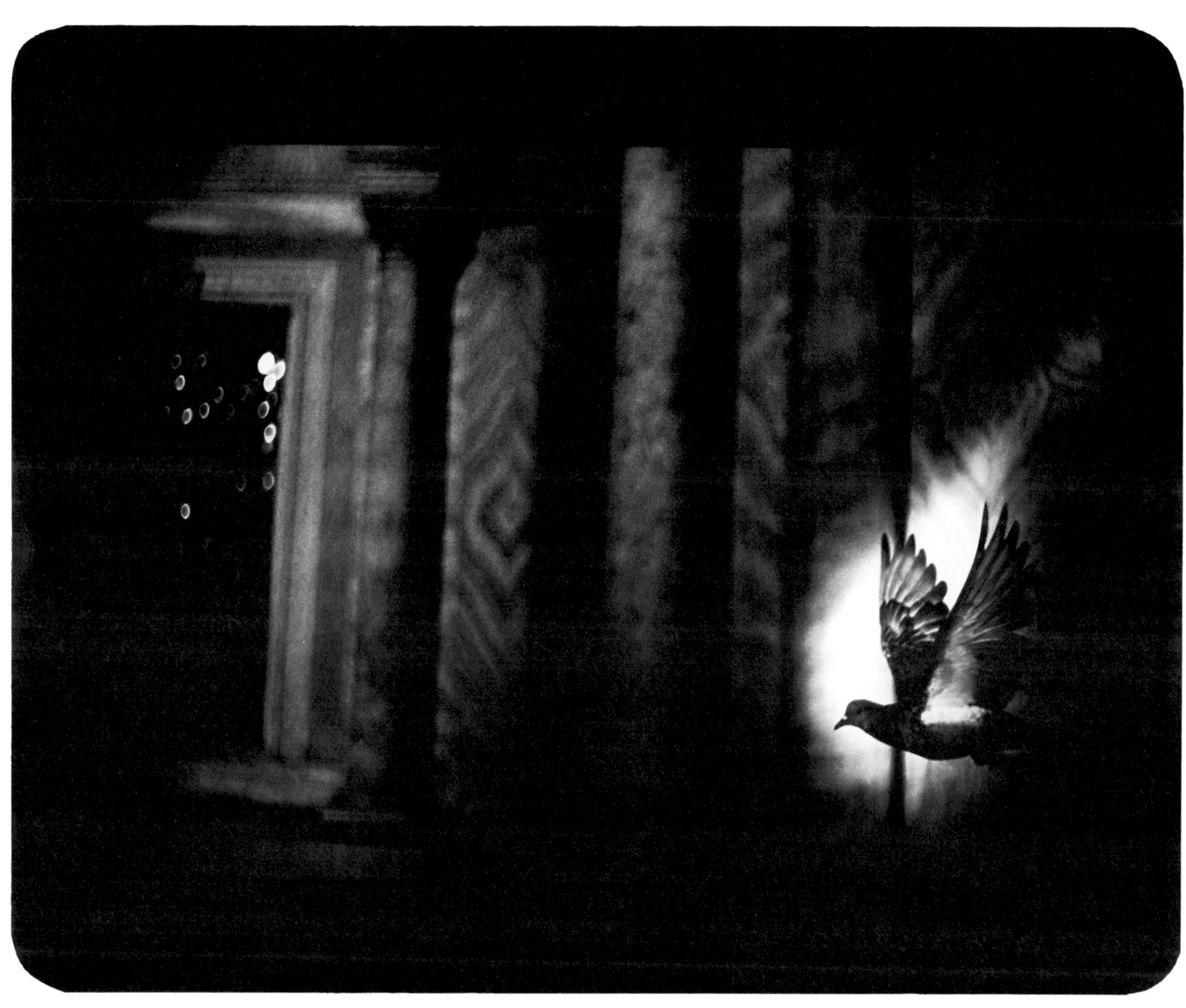

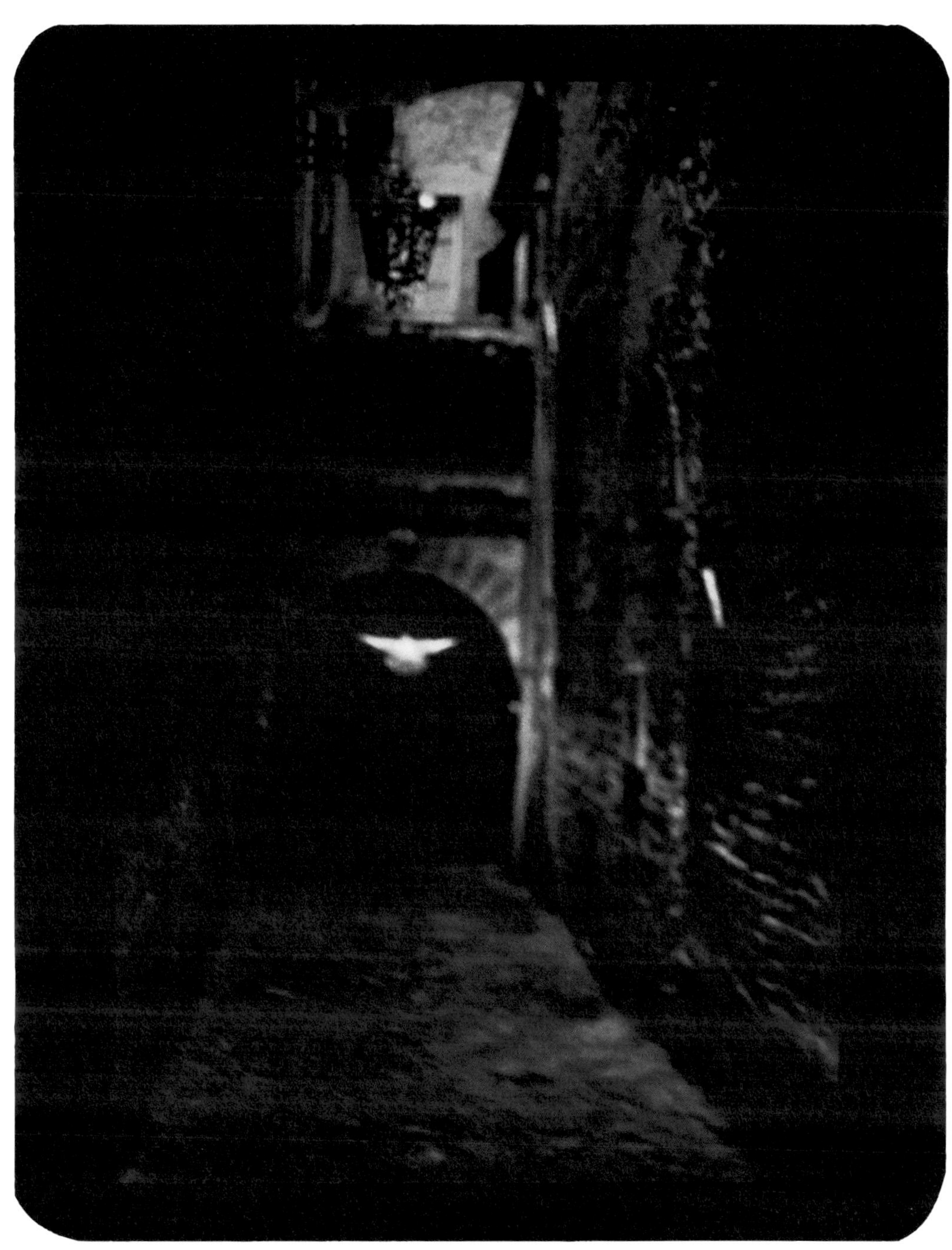

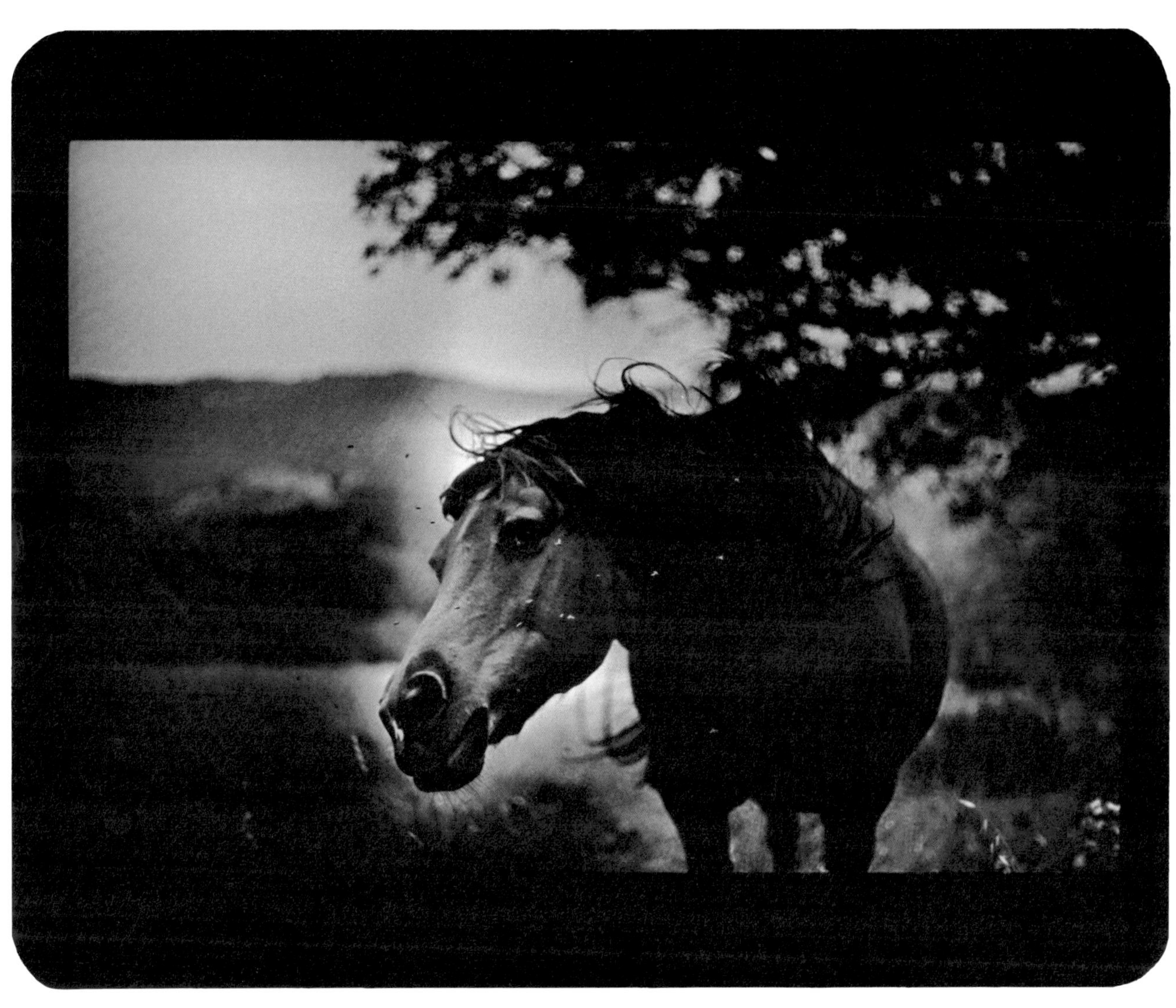

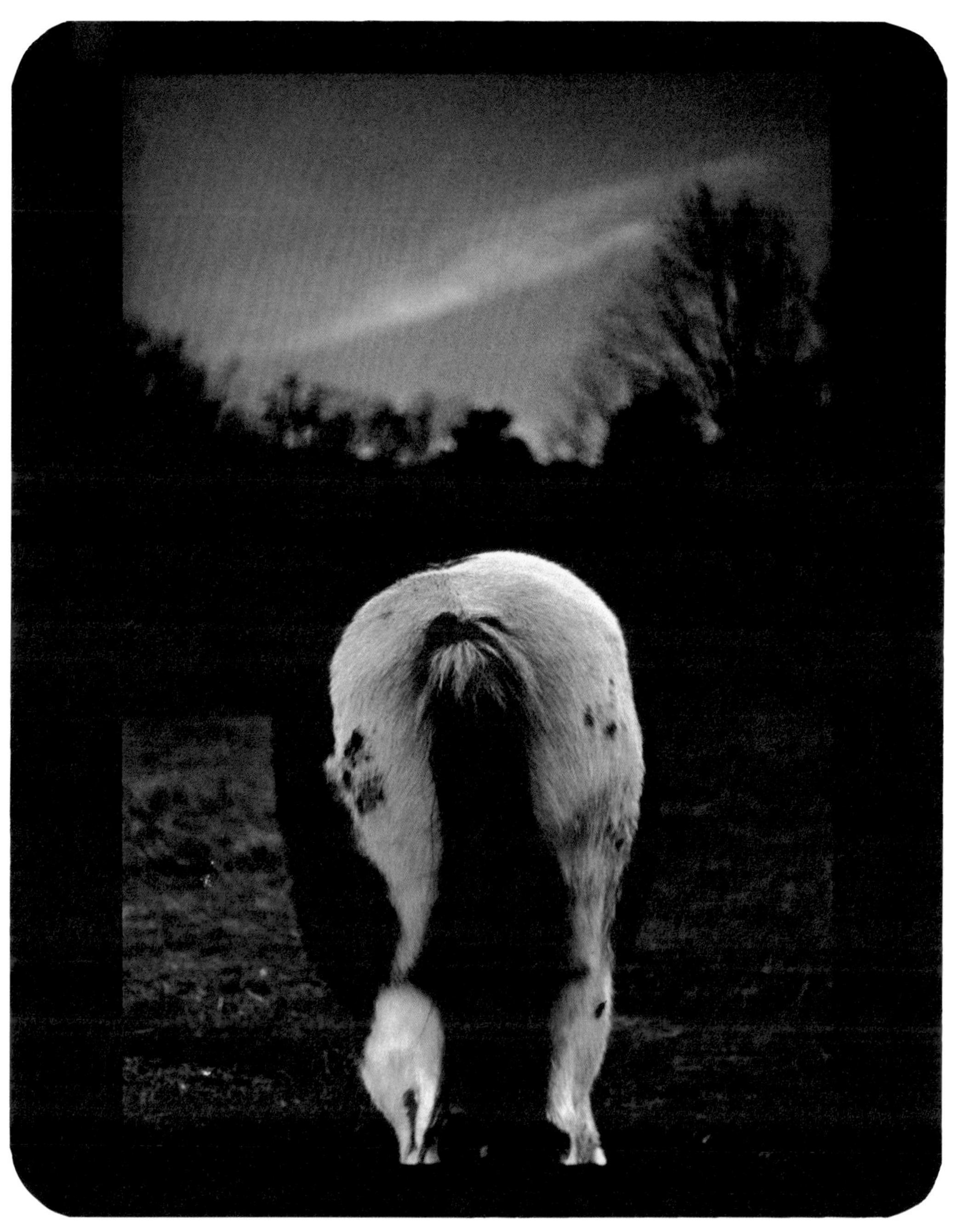

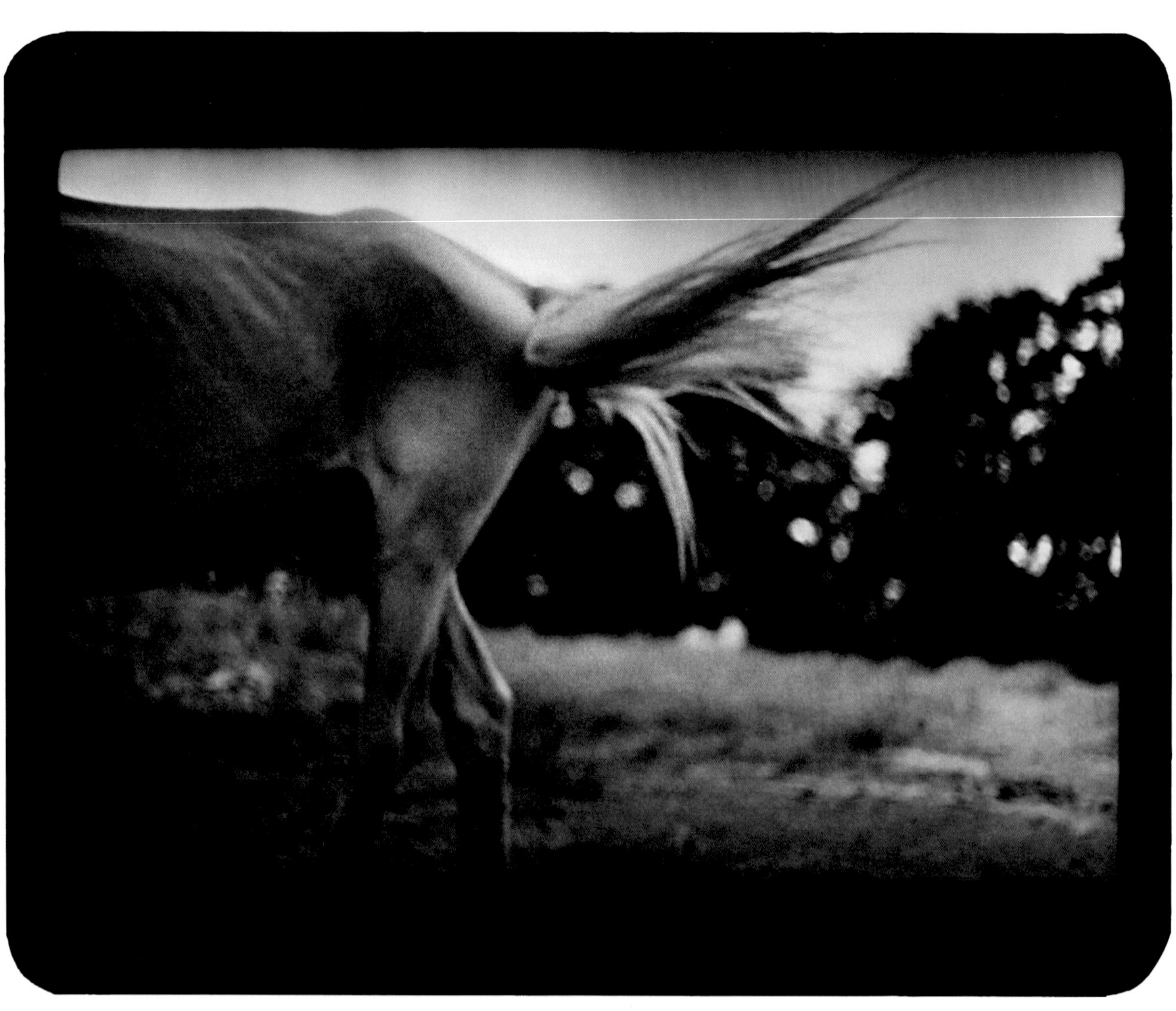

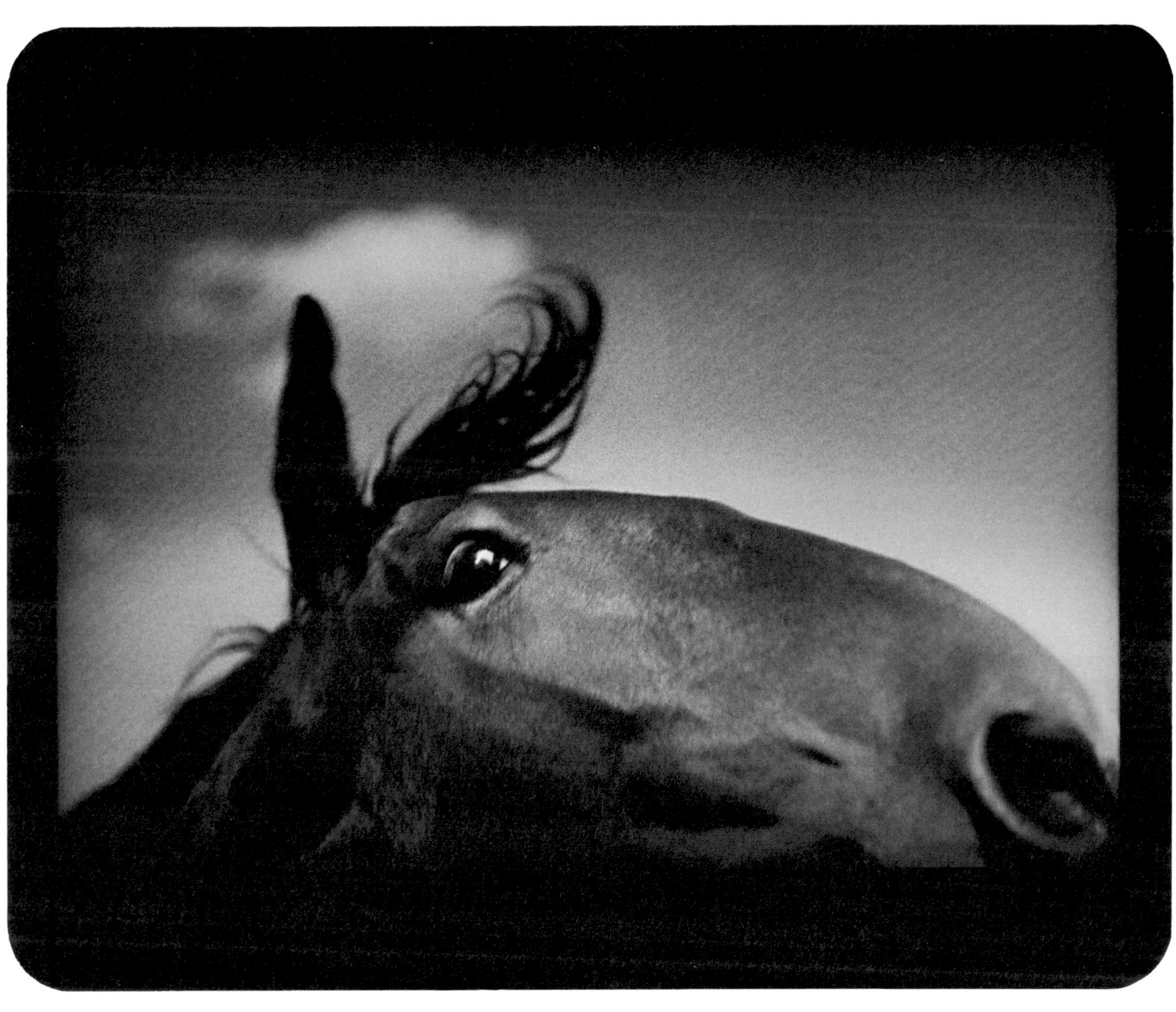

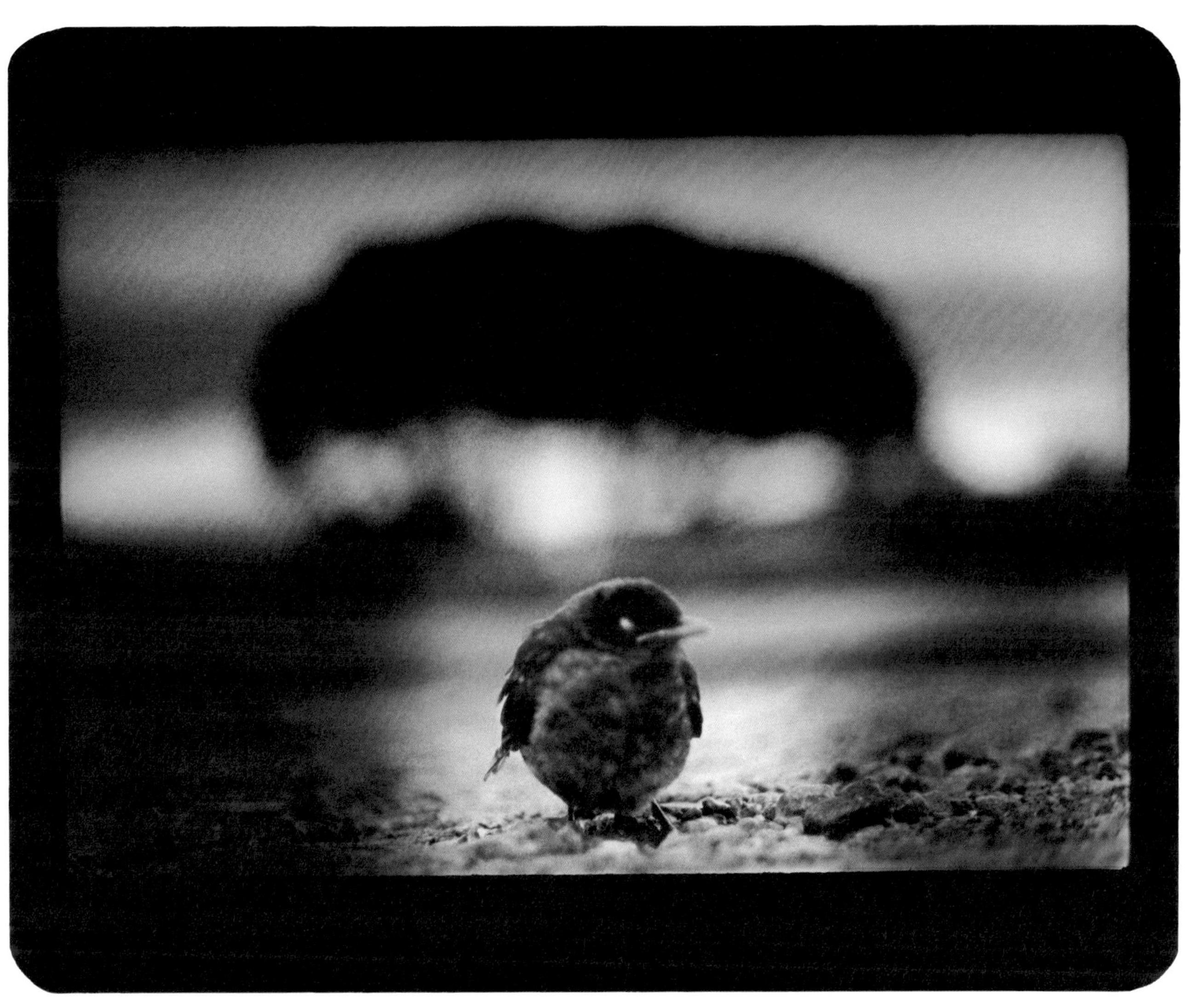

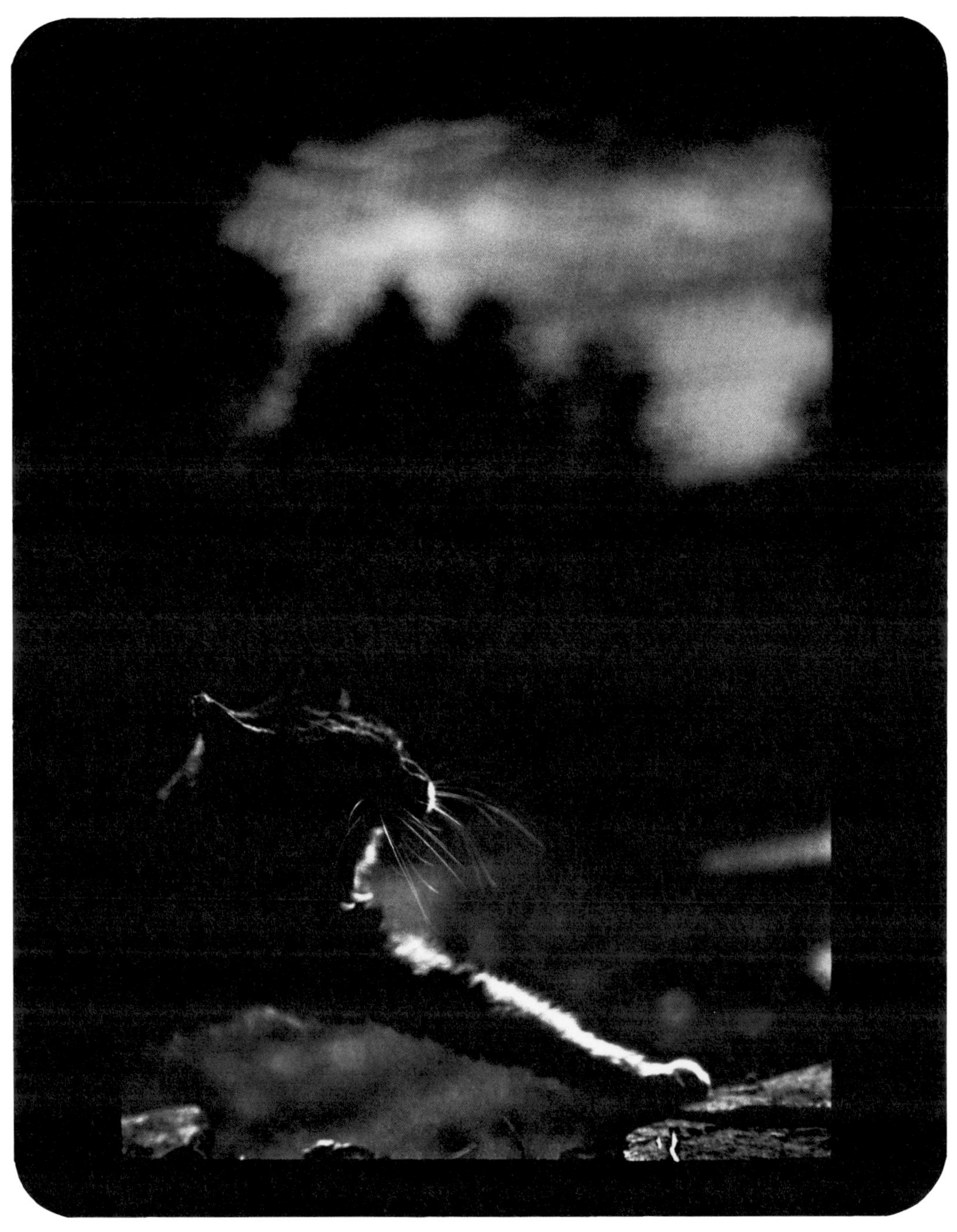

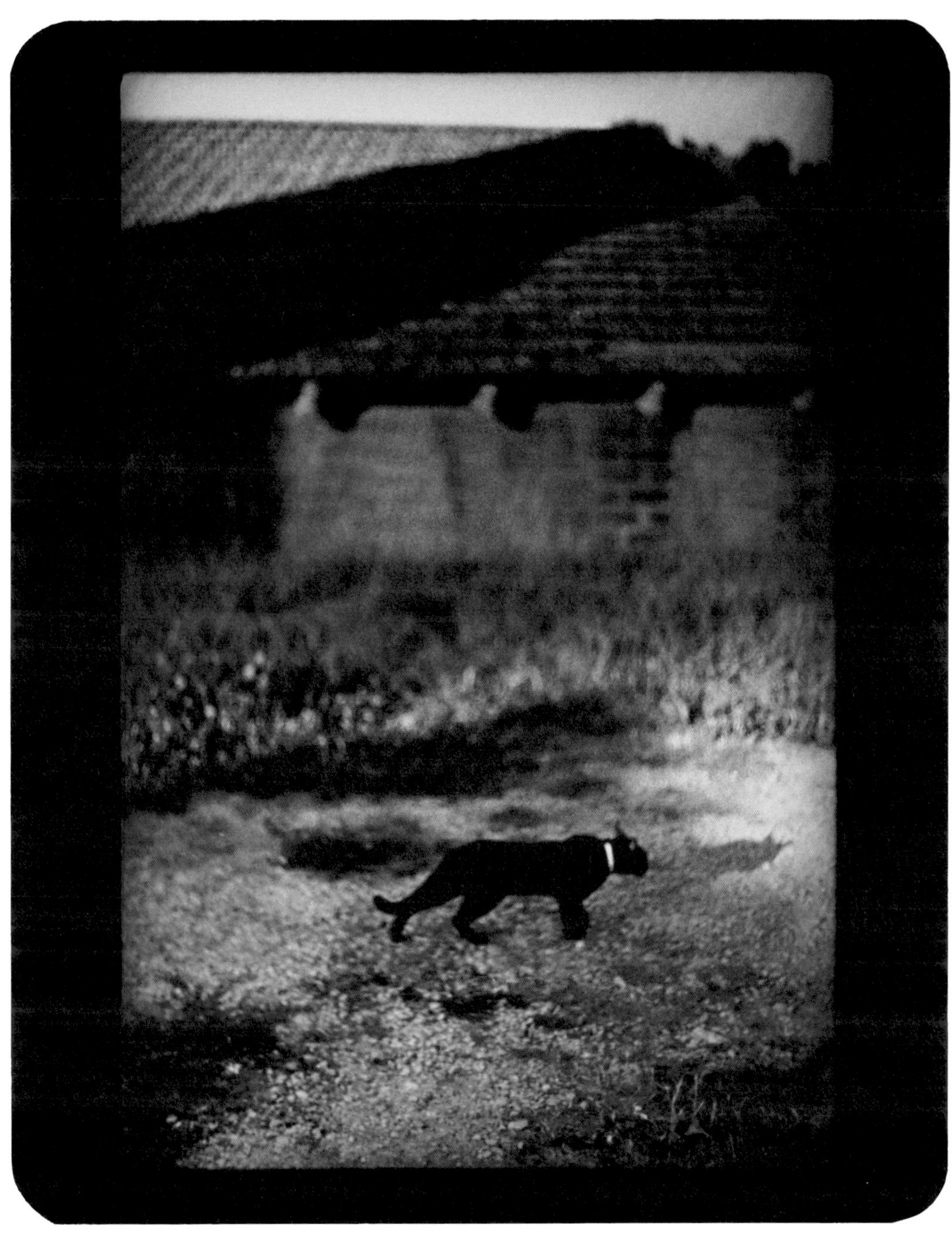

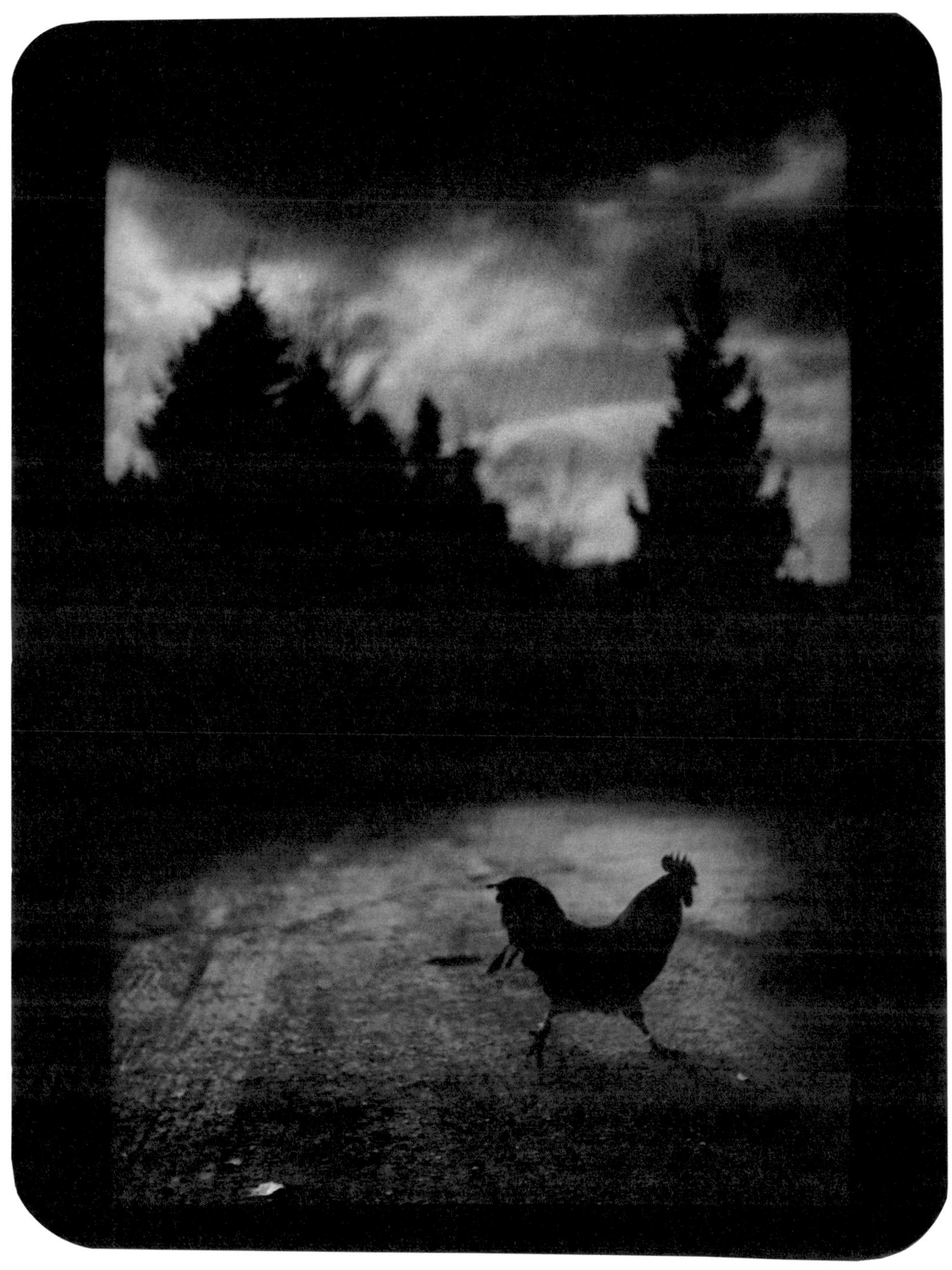

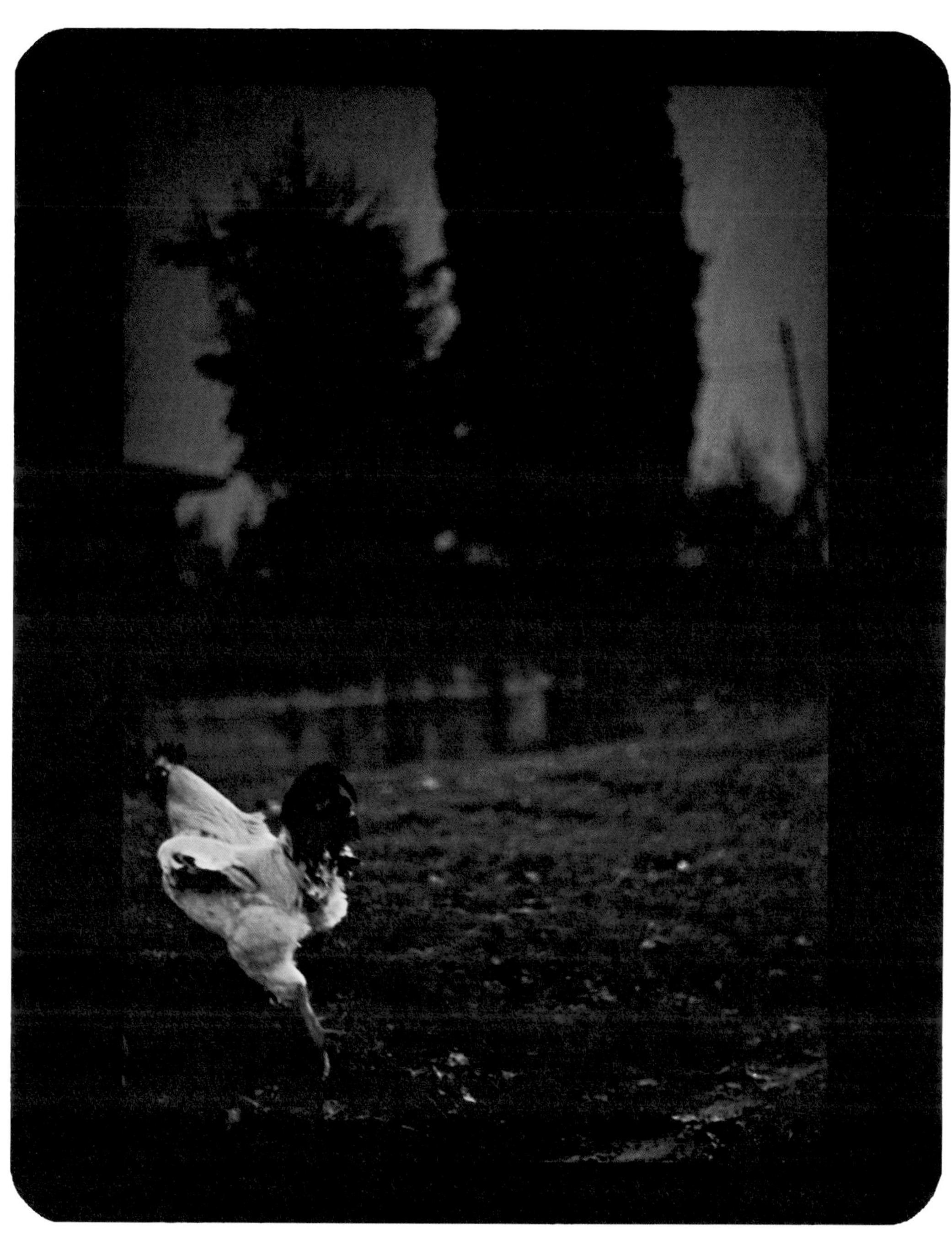

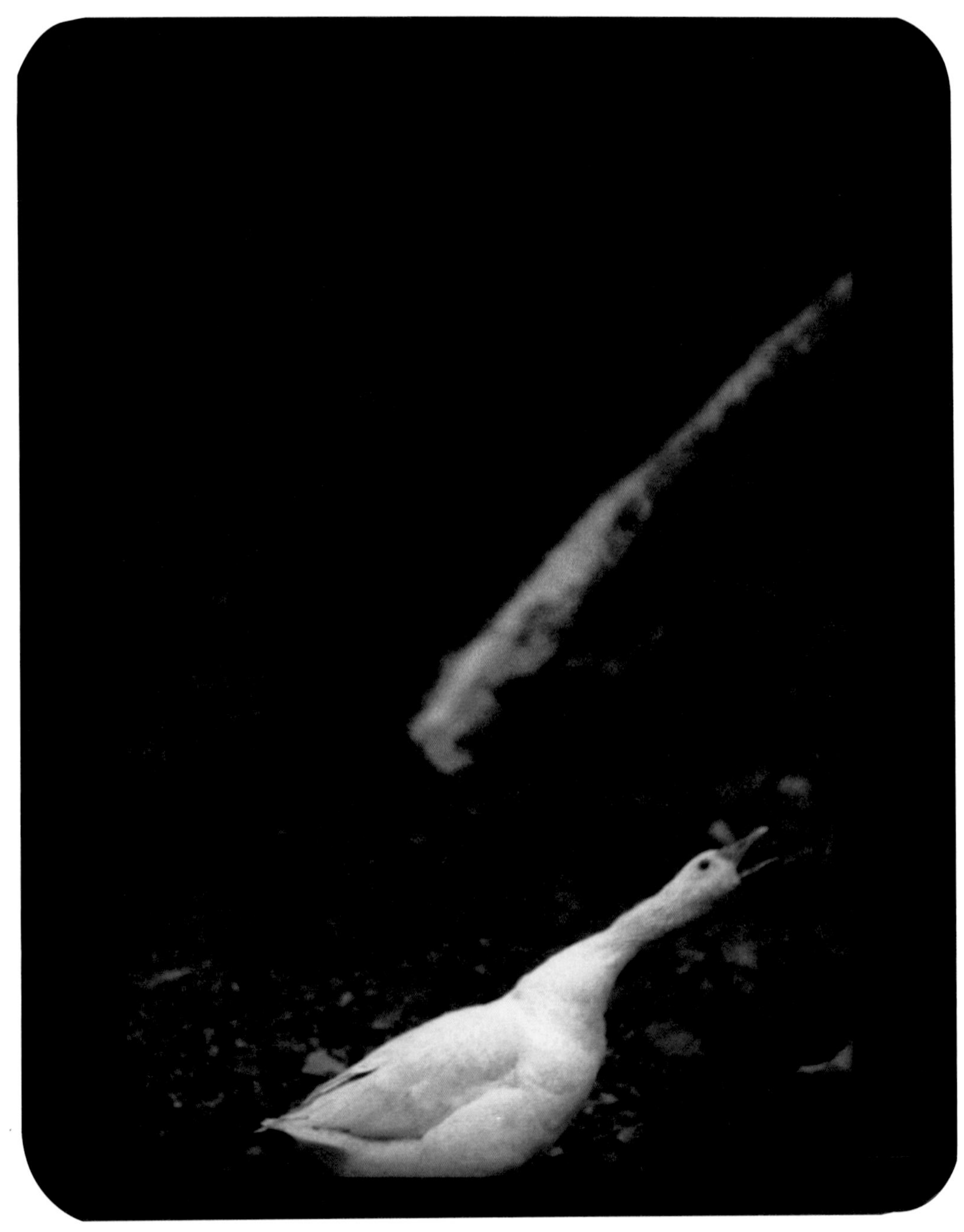

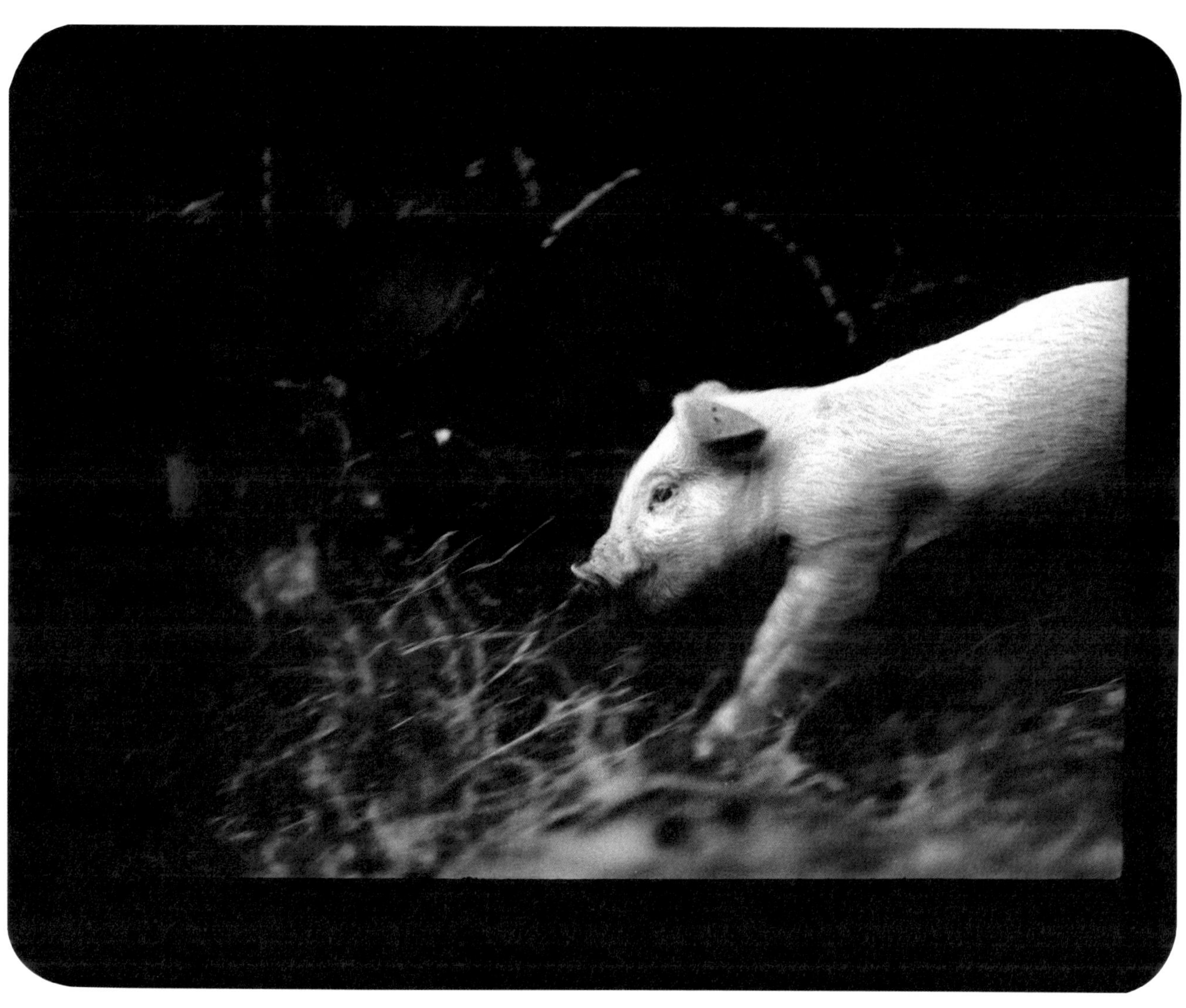

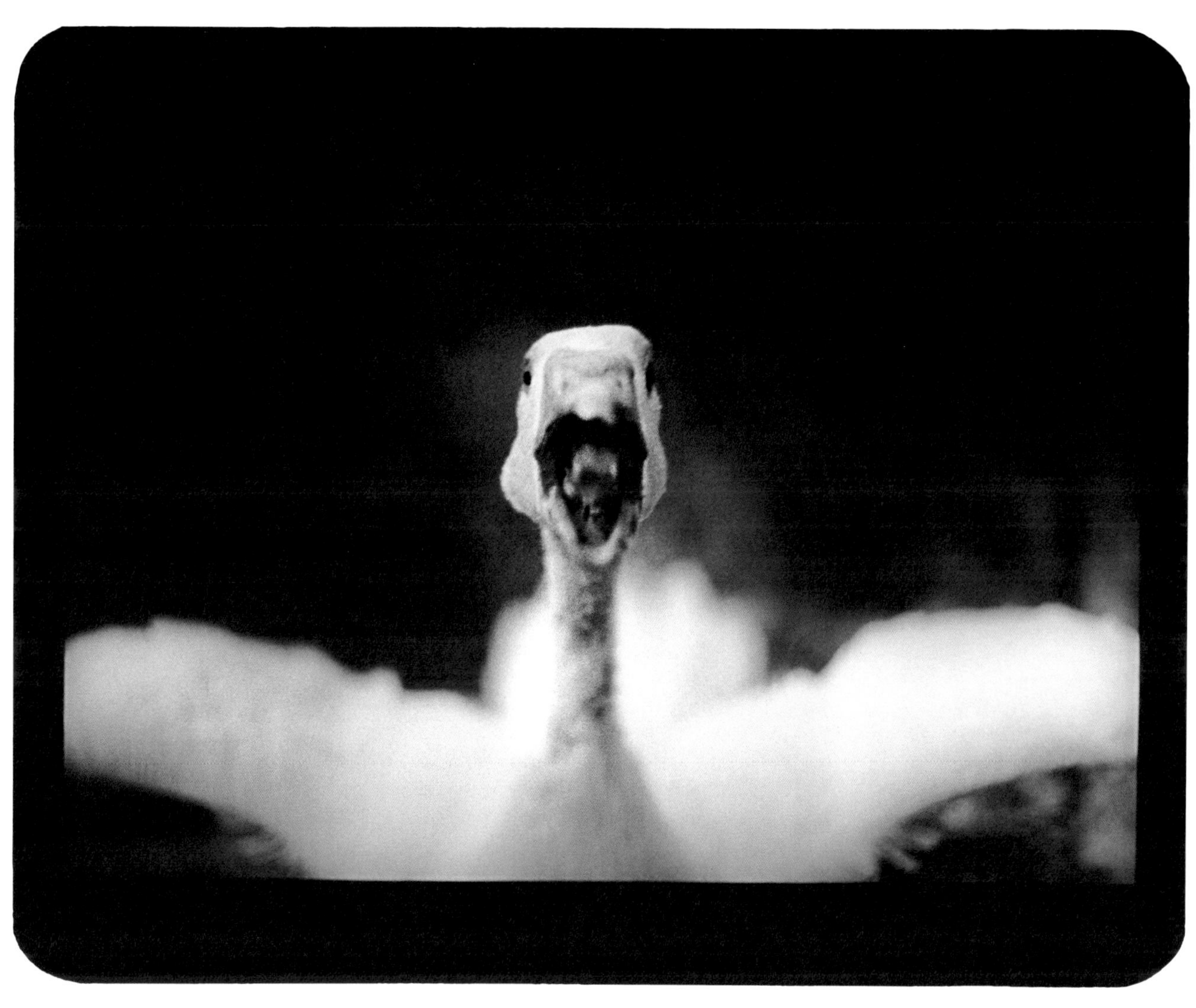

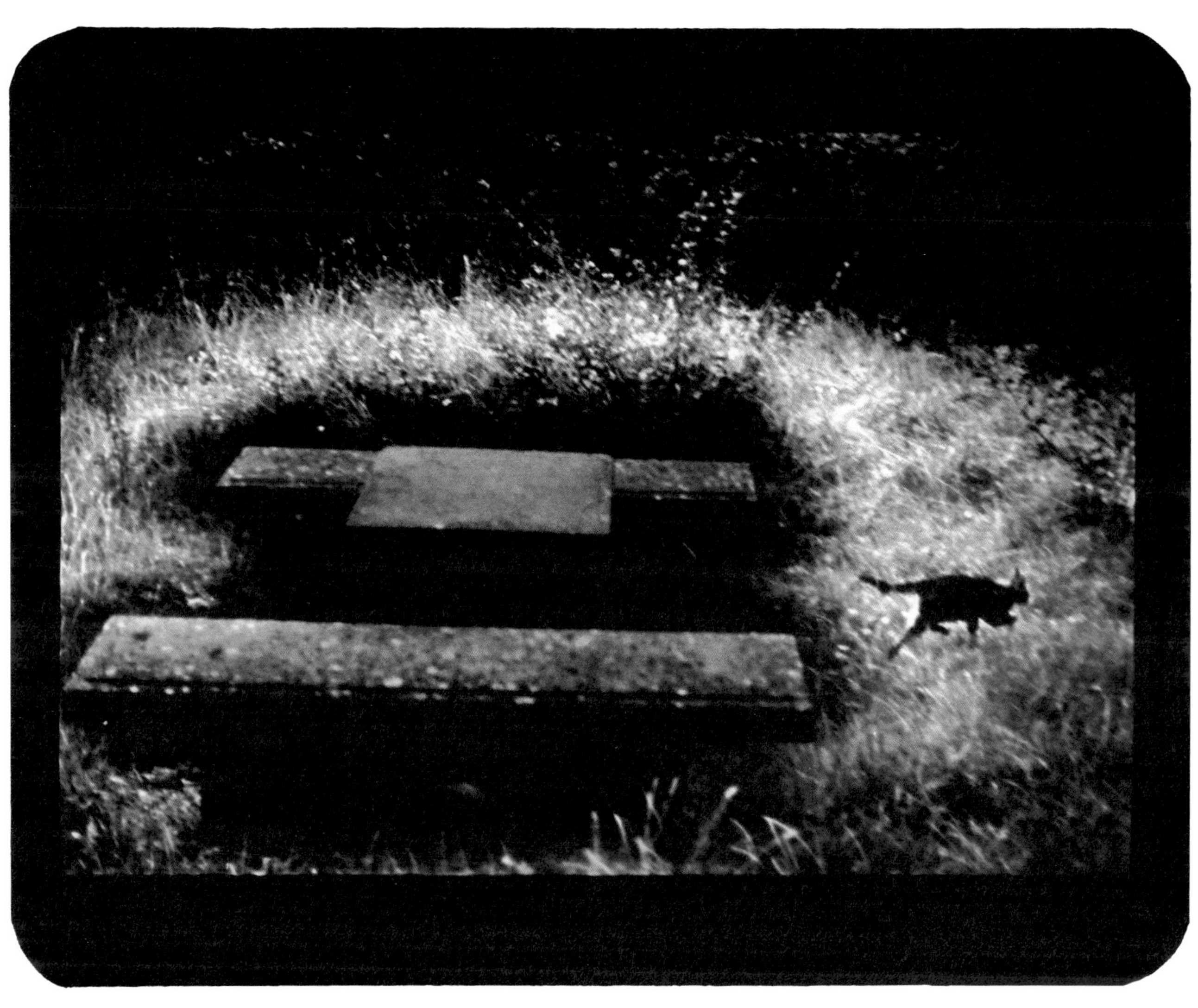

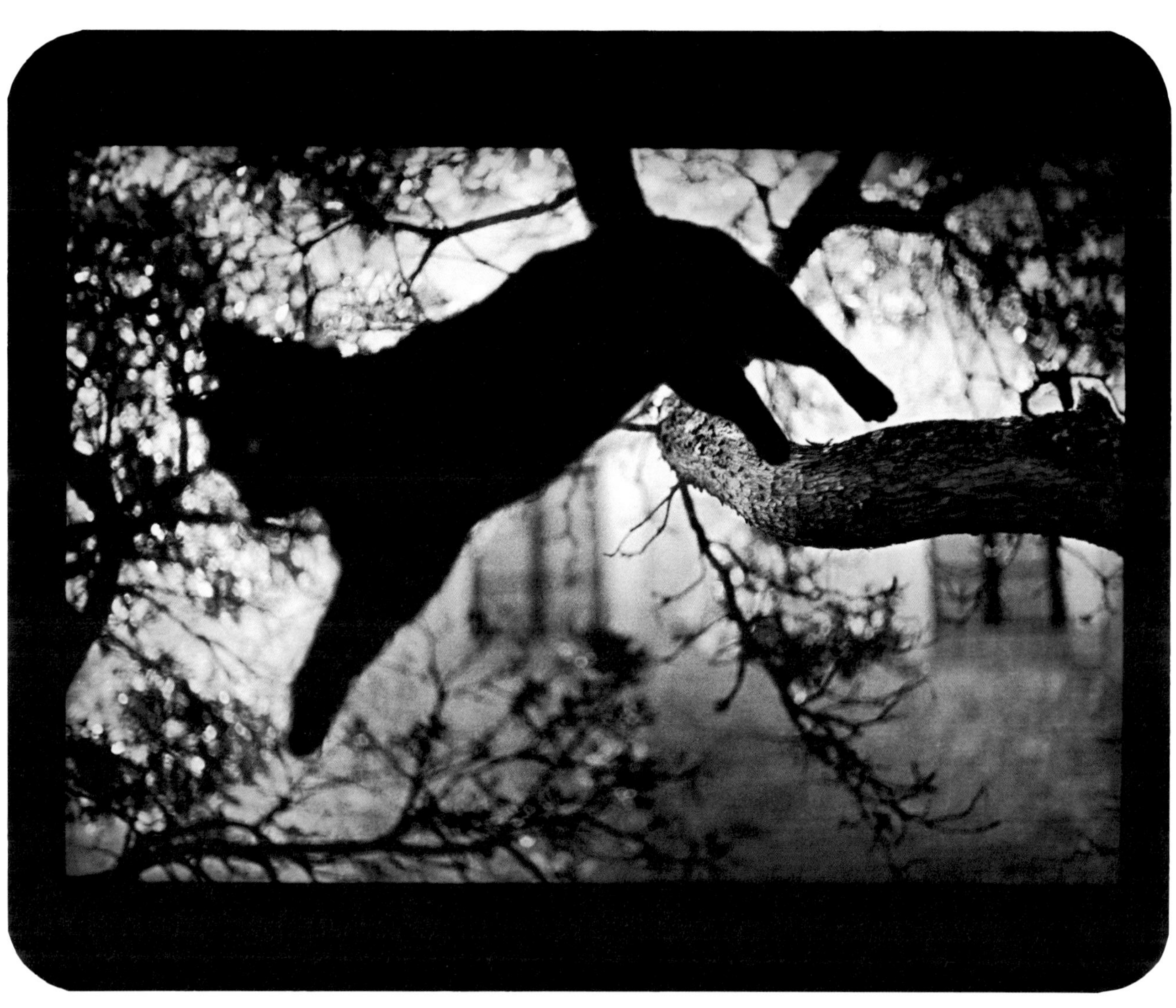

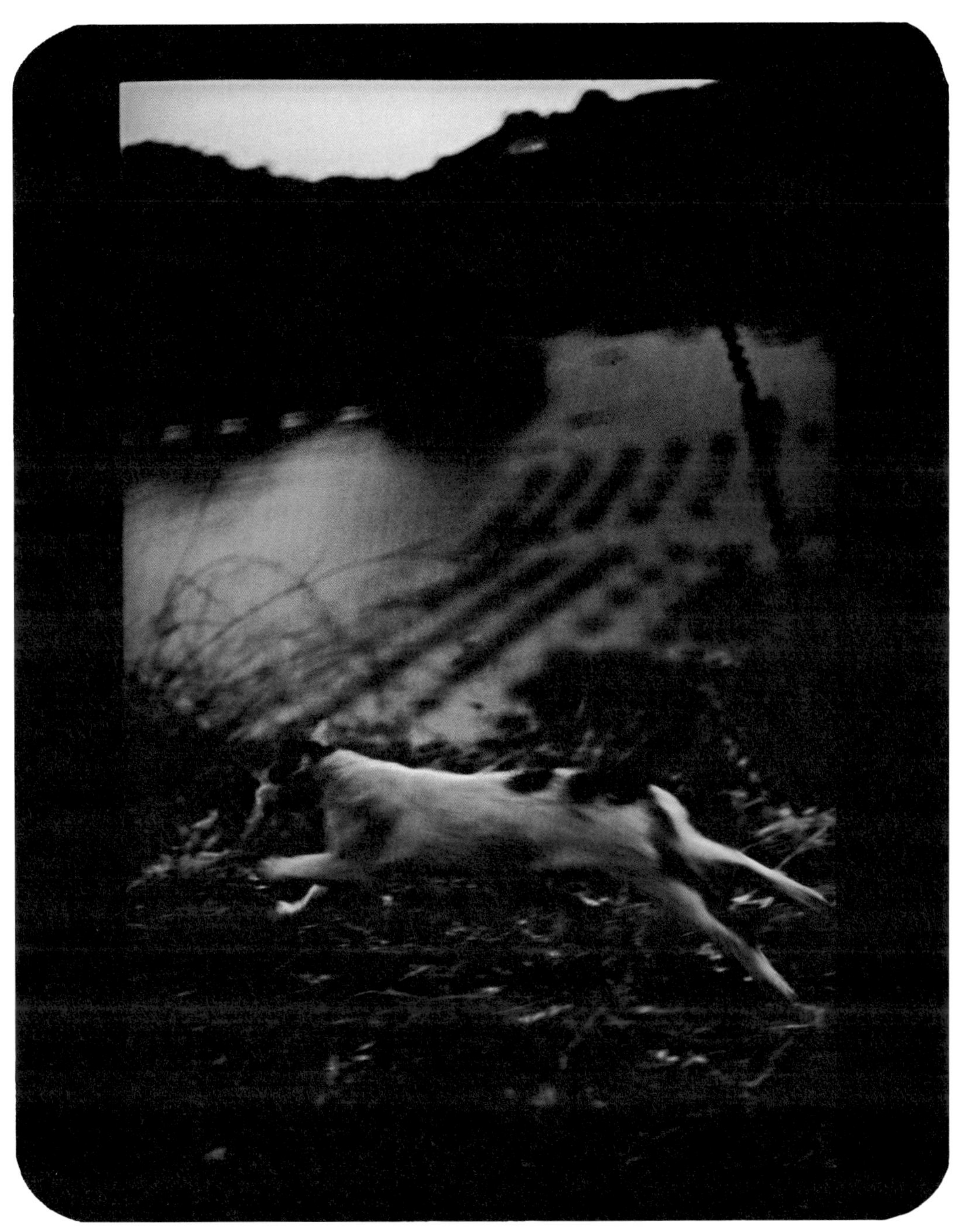

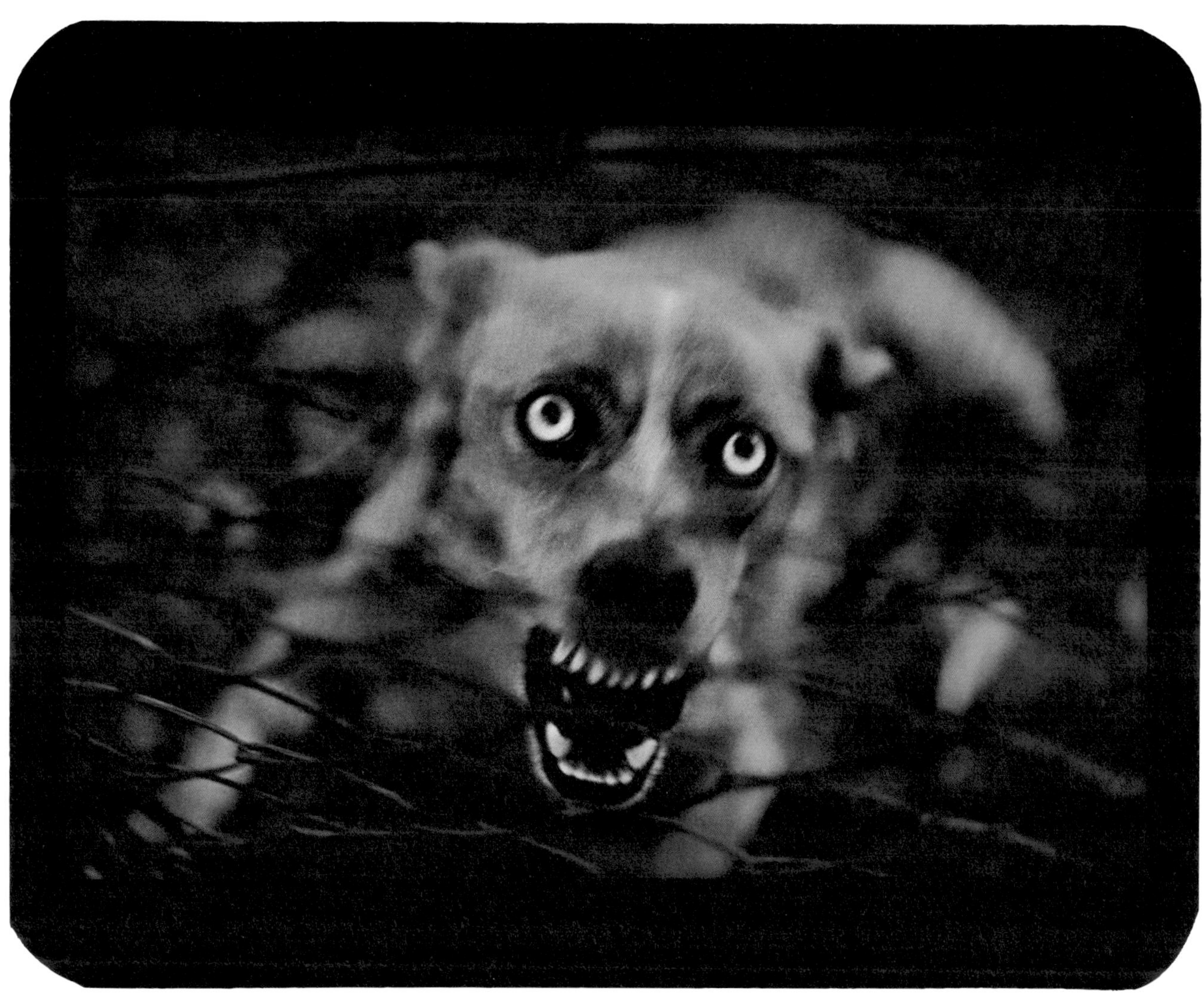

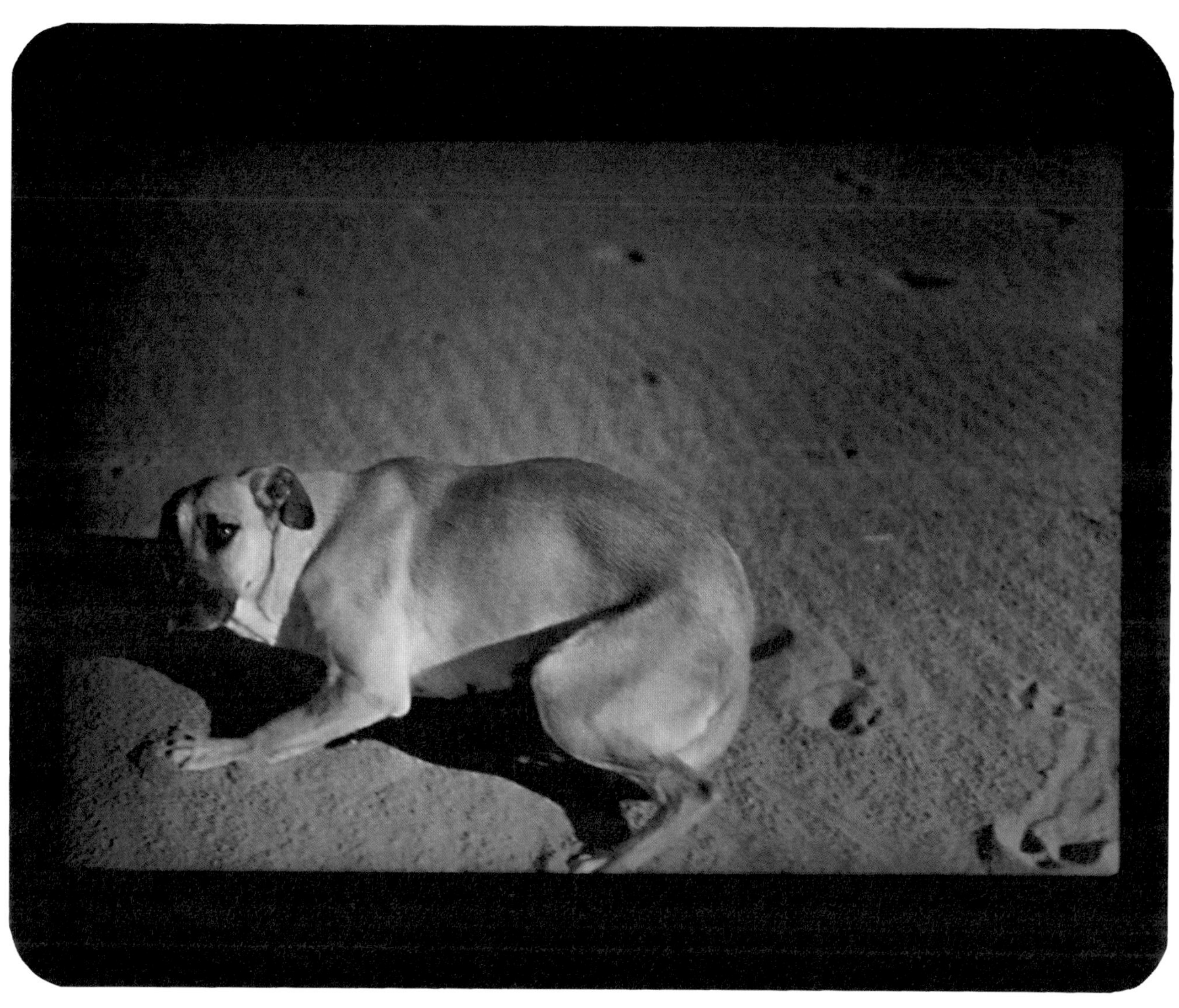

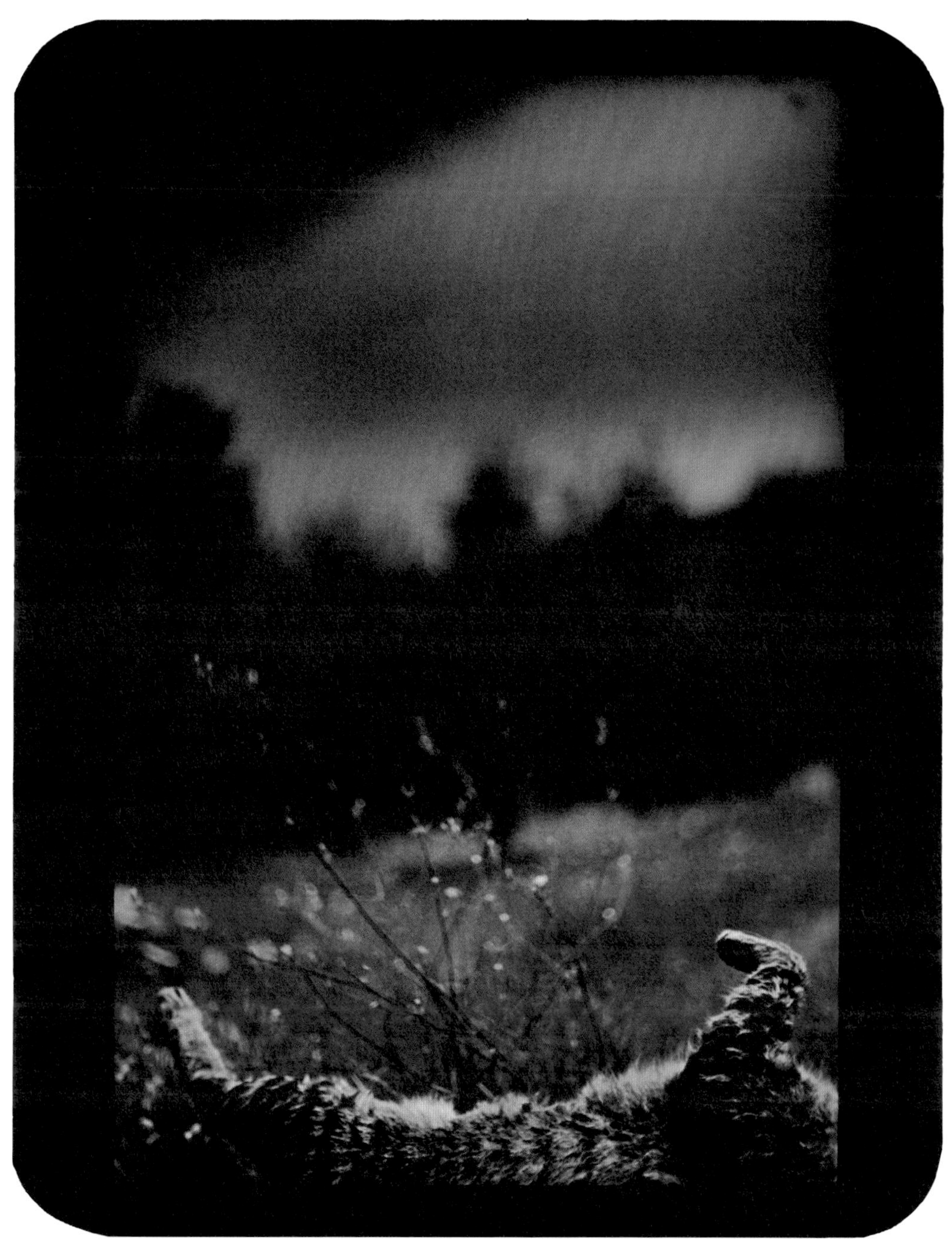

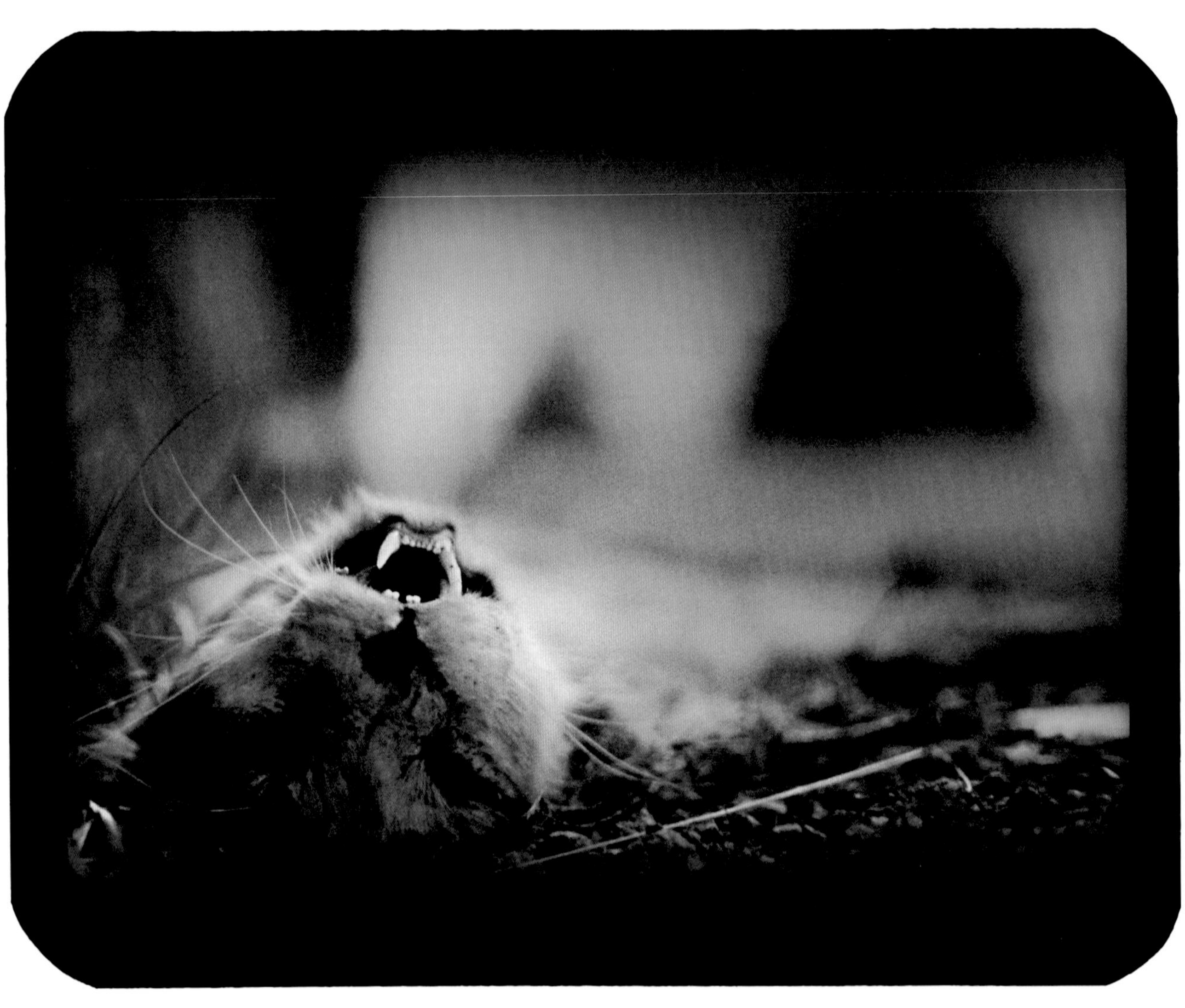

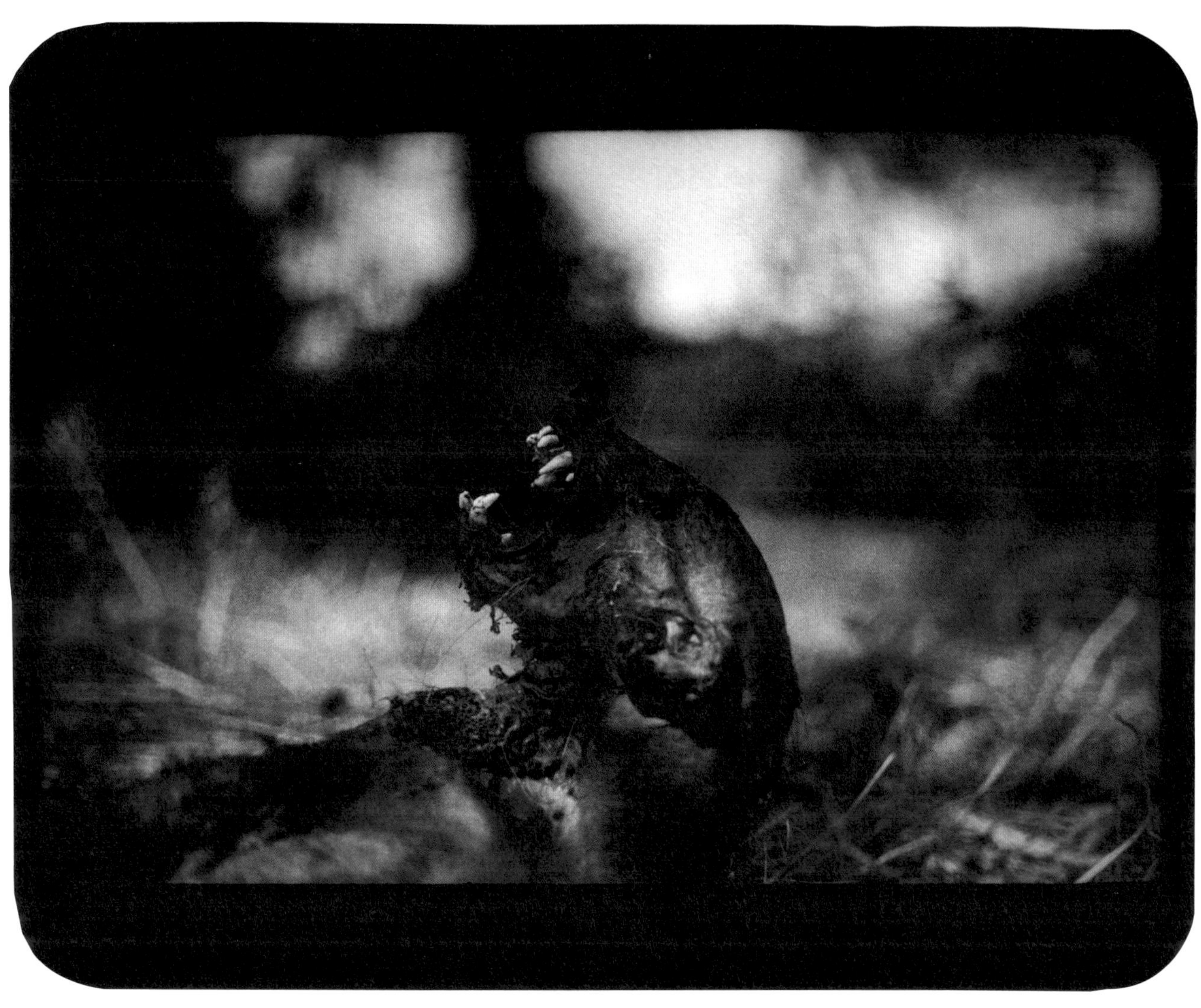

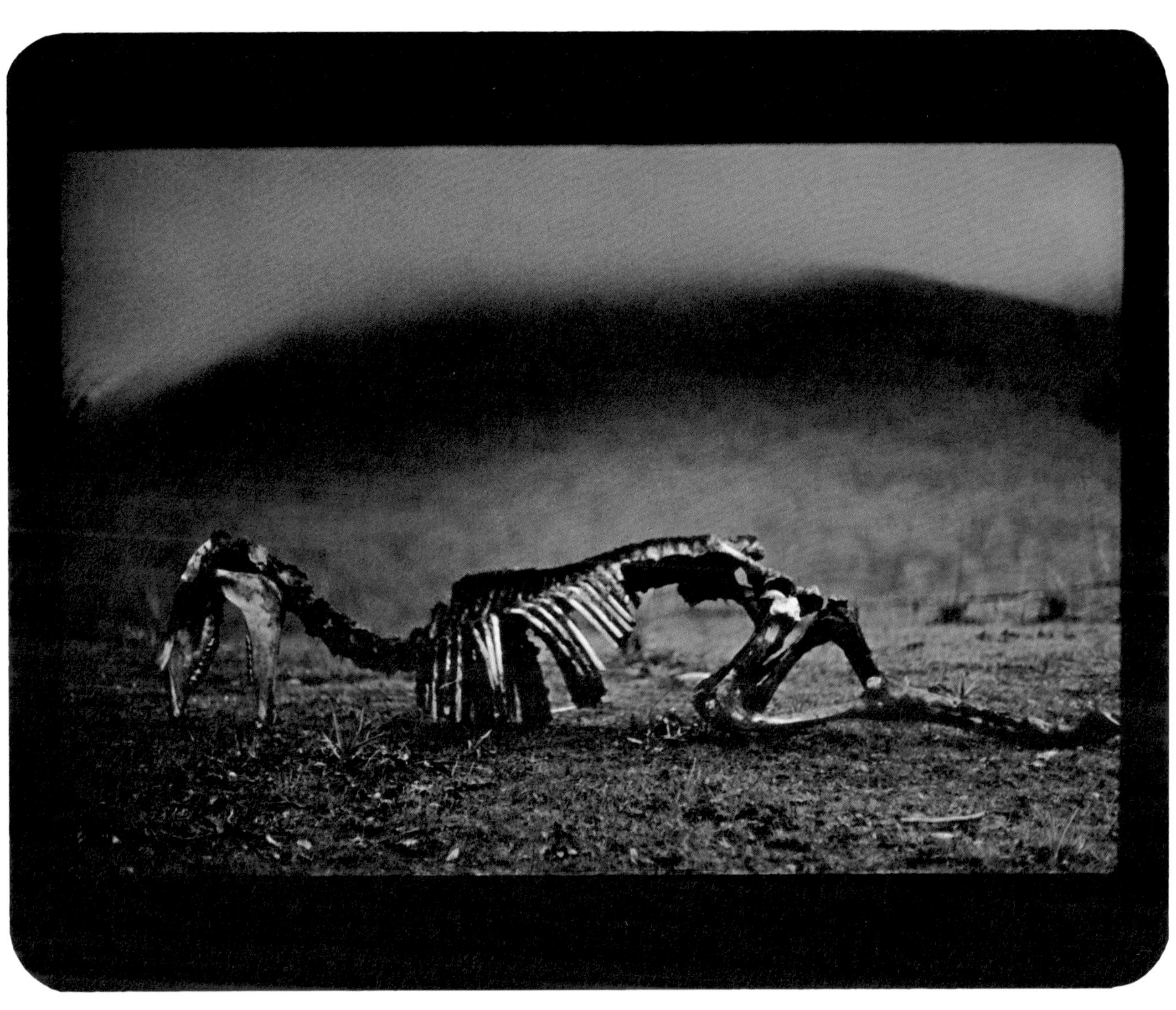

With sincere thanks to
Dewi Lewis
Caroline Warhurst
Peter Fetterman
Alison Nordström

THE ANIMALS
Giacomo Brunelli

This revised edition first published
in the United Kingdom in 2016 by
Dewi Lewis Publishing
8 Broomfield Road
Heaton Moor
Stockport SK4 4ND
England

www.dewilewis.com

ISBN: 978-1-911306-08-5

Design and Layout: Dewi Lewis Publishing
Print: EBS, Verona, Italy

Original edition published by Dewi Lewis Publishing in 2008

www.giacomobrunelli.com